Inclusive Programming for Elementary Students with Autism

Sheila Wagner, M.Ed.

Future Horizons, Inc.

INCLUSIVE PROGRAMMING
FOR ELEMENTARY STUDENTS WITH AUTISM

All marketing and publishing rights guaranteed to and reserved by

FUTURE HORIZONS INC.

721 W. Abram Street
Arlington, Texas 76013
800-489-0727
817-277-0727
817-277-2270 (fax)
E-mail: info@FHautism.com
www.FHautism.com

Cataloging in Publications Data is available from the Library of Congress.

ISBN 1-885477-54-6

Table of Contents

Preface

Congratulations! You are part of an elite group of individuals that is considering (or already conducting) an inclusive programming for students with autism. I hope that you will find this book helpful during your inclusion process. As it is true with any inclusion program for students with severe disabilities, an inclusive program for students with autism takes commitment, enthusiasm, training, support, flexibility and a love of teaching to ensure the best possible educational program for your students.

This book, based on the Emory Autism Resource Center (EARC) model, is for use by schools in educating their students with autism, although parents of children with autism will also benefit by the tips in this book.

I will provide a general overview of inclusion programming for school-age students with autism, as well as a selection of forms on specific programs. You may revise materials in this book at any time. Due to the wide diversity of the autistic disorder, each inclusion program must be developed individually, with the individual student's abilities and characteristics as the guiding factor for the program. Forms may be copied for use in your program, although familiarity with the information in the forms does not promise expertise in this area.

Sheila Wagner, M.Ed.

Acknowledgments

Many people helped to make the EARC Inclusion Project a success over the years, and I would be remiss to not to thank as many people and agencies as possible. Thanks go out to the following people and agencies:

CADEF, Inc., which made many dreams possible with its generous funding.

Janice Hamrick, Ed.D. and Ham Kinsey who saw what was possible.

Clarke, Cobb, Glynn, and Forsyth County Administrations.

To all the current and past inclusion coordinators who work tirelessly to carry out my ideas, as well as develop their own. Their initiative and creativity have been a tremendous asset to the program. Their drive and consistency ensure the longevity of the EARC project:

Kelly Kancel, Lynn Holland, Tina Smith, Christine Norris, Marcy Brewer,

Debbie Griffith, Christine Marcant, Heather Vining, Jody Sweeney, and Alice Morrison.

And to their schools:

Sixes Elementary, Barnett Shoals Elementary, Mountain View Elementary,

Mt. Bethel Elementary, Baker Elementary, Dowell Elementary,

Golden Isles Elementary, Glendale Elementary,

Chattahoochee Elementary, and

Vickery Creek Elementary

To my EARC in-school liaisons, who, with their patience, enthusiasm, excitement, and willingness to learn new strategies and teach others, make the entire project possible. They have the ability to change the world and the drive to accomplish it:

Christi Bianchi, Amy Reilly, and especially Brooke Ingersoll,

who assisted in the production of the original booklet.

Thanks, Brooke! I couldn't have done it without you.

Most importantly, thanks go to all of the students with autism that have participated, in one way or another, in this program. Watching them grow and learn cements the belief that every moment is worth all the effort.

Credit also goes to the countless teachers and professors who have come up with the original strategies that are used with students with autism. Most of them are in such common use in everyday teaching that it is difficult to find the original source. We had used many strategies that we felt could be modified for the student's benefit and made them work in the regular education setting. Some were mistakes; some were ingenious. Sometimes there was little difference between the two. To all those that originally discovered that a particular strategy might work with someone with autism, thank you.

Thanks also, to my boss, Gail G. McGee, Ph.D., who gives me the freedom to spread my wings and explore the world of educating students with autism. She doesn't know how much fun my job is! Finally, thanks to my family, who has had to learn to live with a workaholic!

Dedication

to Matt and Eric
because they keep forcing us to consider
pushing the envelope of inclusion,

to Mary Margaret
whose clarity and articulation helps this "NT"
to better understand this disorder,

and to Nancy Dalrymple
who had no idea what she was starting.

Introduction

In the fall of 1993, EARC received a grant from the Childhood Autism Diagnostic and Educational Foundation, Inc. (CADEF) to address the needs of school-age students with autism within the regular education setting. Across the nation, educational programming for students with severe disabilities had responded to the more inclusive philosophies garnered by researchers such as Wayne Sailor, Rob Horner, Gail McGee, Phil Strain, and many others. However, little research had been conducted with school-age students with autism in inclusive settings. To address this need, the EARC began its Inclusion Project for students with autism, funded through CADEF. The project began in the spring of 1994 in Cherokee County, Georgia (a Metro-Atlanta county) with six students with autism or related disorders. Each year, this project has expanded to involve new counties in Georgia. As a result of this ongoing project, more students with autism join the growing ranks of students who are included with their typically developing peers. By the end of the 1997-98 school term, this intensive program followed more than 97 students.

Teachers and parents of students with autism have seen much success and progress as a result of this project.

Inclusion Philosophy

Inclusive Programming for Students with Autism

What's the Reason Behind It?

Research has documented that non-handicapped peers can be effective in teaching social skills for students with autism. The most effective methods for addressing the students with autism in inclusive settings include play activities that have been appropriately structured, when the peers receive training, and the teachers actively prompt and then reinforce the interactions between the student with autism and the peers.

(Strain, Shores, & Timm, 1977; Odom, Hoyson, Jamieson, & Strain, 1985; Roeyers, H., 1996)

There is currently a strong educational movement to integrate students with autism and other disabilities with their general education peers.

(Kamps, D.M.; Barbetta, P.M., and Leonard, B.R.; and Delquadri, J., 1994)

Research suggests that successful integration depends on the careful planning, development, and implementation of programs that emphasize both the academic and the social needs of students with disabilities.

(Kamps, D.M.;Barbetta, P.M.,and Leonard, B.R.; and Delquadri, J., 1994; Gaylord-Ross, 1989; Gresham, 1986; Sailor et al., 1989)

Recently, educational placement options for children with autism have expanded in response to changing theories of programming for all special needs children. Many children with autism are now enjoying placement options in regular education classrooms and are learning with their typical peers. The benefits of this type of placement are clear, although the programming must be well defined and implemented in order to increase the likelihood of success. Many issues must be considered when implementing an inclusion program for any child with special needs, and for a child with autism, in particular. The model adopted by the EARC Inclusion Project incorporates a number of strategies to aid in regular educational placement. The essential aspects of this project are presented in order for school systems to gain a better understanding of the components that we believe are necessary for a successful program for children with autism.

Benefits to children with autism

Children with autism have pronounced impairments in social and communication development that hinder their interactions with peers and family members. They often behave inappropriately when faced with social situations, resulting in negative opinions among their peers. When a child with autism does not have access to adaptive role models, progress toward improving social and communication skills is often hampered. Regular education can offer valuable opportunities for social interactions with peers. However, placement in regular education alone does not ensure success.

Children with autism require supports to help them develop and generalize necessary social skills. With adequate supports in place, significant improvements in social interactions can occur.

Benefits to typical children

Typical peers also benefit from participation in an inclusion program by developing a heightened awareness of the needs of children with disabilities. This can lead to greater sensitivity toward others and acceptance of the relative strengths and weaknesses that we all have. Many parents acknowledge these benefits of inclusive programming.

Benefits of peer tutoring/social skills programming

Teachers have long recognized the additional benefits that peer influence has on teaching academics and on the student's self-esteem. However, for students with autism, the mere presence of typical models is not sufficient for learning more subtle skills, such as those found in the social domain. Recently, both professionals and parents have begun to recognize the major impact positive models can have for children with disabilities such as autism. When formal peer tutor programs, with a strong foundation of social skills, are used for direct teaching of both social and language skills, the students with disabilities benefit. Students who experience difficulty with peer interactions or reciprocal conversations are presented with numerous opportunities in which peers frequently and repeatedly request appropriate responses from them. This provides the students with the best environment to develop skills in both the social and language domains under the guidance of a teacher.

With consistent and frequent exposure to peer programs, teachers and parents report the students gain increased language production, decreased solitary play, and increased appropriate play skills. One parent related that for the first time he watched his son play with his brothers, something that he had not seen prior to the peer influence in the school setting. A teacher watched a child's independent play go from walking the perimeter of the building to becoming part of the group of children playing at recess time.

Teachers and parents have begun to recognize that it is extremely difficult for adults to teach age-appropriate social skills to a child. However, children often readily learn these skills from another child, making peer tutor programs and social skills training important, especially during the school years. These programs are well worth investigating for any teacher with students who have social or language difficulties, such as autism.

References

Gaylord-Ross, R. J. (1989). *Integration Strategies for Students with Handicaps.* Baltimore: Brookes.

Gresham, F.M. (1986). Strategies for enhancing the social outcomes of mainstreaming: A necessary ingredient for success. In C. J. Meisel (Ed), *Mainstreaming handicapped children: Outcomes, Controversies, and New Directions* (pp. 193-218). Hillsdale, NJ: Erlbaum.

Sailor, W., Anderson, J.L., Halvorsen, A.T., Doering, K., Filler, J.. & Geotz, L. (1989). *The comprehensive local school: Regular education for all students with disabilities.* Baltimore: Brookes.

Kamps, D., Barbetta, P.M., & Delquadri, J. (1994). Classwide peer tutoring: An integration strategy to improve reading skills and promote peer interactions among students with autism and general education peers. *Journal of Applied Behavior Analysis.* 27, 49-61.

Odom, S.L., Hoyson, M., Jamieson, B., & Strain, P.S. (1985). Increasing handicapped preschoolers peer social interactions: Cross-setting and component analysis. *Journal of Applied Behavior Analysis,* 18, 3-16

Roeyers, H. (1996). The influence of nonhandicapped peers on the social interactions of children with a pervasive developmental disorder. *Journal of Autism and Developmental Disorders,* 26, 303-320.

Strain, P.S. Shores, R.E. & Timm, M.A. (1977). Effects of peers social initiations on the behavior of withdrawn preschool children. *Journal of Applied Behavior Analysis,* 10, 188-198.

Inclusion Project Rationale

Children with disabilities lose many opportunities for pleasurable experiences and friendships because of the misconceptions adults and the children's peers have about them. Philosophies on how to teach children with special needs have changed since Public Law 94-142 was passed (Aloia, Beaver, & Pettus, 1978). The philosophies have ranged from completely segregated schools and classrooms, to partial participation, to partial mainstreaming, to peer tutor programs, to reverse mainstreaming, or to full or partial inclusion. Often, the only difference between philosophies is found in the definition of the different programs (Wooten, M. & Mesibov, G.B., 1986).

After much consideration, debate and years, it is clear that the children with disabilities are the ones who are often the forgotten factor when philosophies clash. Too many children have lost, or are losing, the opportunities of meeting their typically developing classmates while the debate rages around them. Research shows that exposure to typical peers enhances social development; allows for opportunities to model positive role models in the classroom, the playground and in the community; elevates self-esteem; and educates typically developing children about their disabled classmates. With training, negative behaviors decrease in the presence of positive behaviors and increase, or stay the same, without support or training for the child with the disability or the regular education classmate (Wooten, M., & Mesibov, G. B., 1986). Children with disabilities should be placed in settings where the positive behaviors can be modeled and training can occur. This is in the regular education setting.

The likelihood of failure is greater when the child with the disability is placed within the regular education setting with no backup support, no specialized training of the teachers, and no education of the typical classmates (Gresham, F.M. 1982). Children in regular education classes tend to be overly critical. They often have negative feelings and offer no opportunities for friendship to the disabled child if they do not understand the reasons for the behaviors (Gresham, F.M., 1982). Some children with disabilities, such as autism, vision impairment, or hearing impairment, often appear to be physically and intellectually at age-level, but can have bizarre and surprising behaviors resulting from their disability that can alienate other children. Research shows that when regular education children receive information about the disabilities, are given the chance to act as "peer tutors"or "buddies," and have the full support of their teacher in times of confusion and frustration, the acceptance of the child with the disability increases dramatically (Goldstein & Ferrell, 1987; Goldstein & Wichstrom, 1986).

The EARC Inclusion Project offers the regular education student the opportunity to learn about children with disabilities; specifically, children with autism. Teachers and staff receive training, information and hands-on-demonstration to aid in their inclusion program. The students in the regular education settings also receive information about the strengths and weaknesses in all people. The goal in offering information to the children is to build future peer tutor programs, offer friendship clubs, enhance the knowledge of the children and staff about disabilities, and to improve the lives of children who have traditionally had little or no opportunity for social involvement.

Necessary Components for the Inclusion Project

Inclusive Philosophy

The belief that all students with autism need and deserve opportunities to learn along with their typical peers is the philosophy from which all aspects of the inclusion project must stem. All teachers who choose to participate in the program should be supportive of the overarching principle of inclusive education for children with disabilities. They should be enthusiastic about the program, flexible in their teaching styles, and positive in their attitude regarding behavior management and social skills interventions. It is most important to provide potential teachers with ample information regarding the objectives and expectations of the program. Voluntary participation is highly recommended.

Administrative Support

In order for inclusion programs to be successful, you must have the full support of the school administration and the Division of Special Education. It is particularly important for the teachers involved in the program to receive support in the form of assistance with scheduling, program consultation, problem-solving, and constructive feedback. Moral support and acknowledgment are also important. Inclusion program participants often experience isolation and burnout when they do not have such support.

Teacher Training

All participating teachers will need training on the characteristics of autism, social skills programming, behavior management, and teaching strategies useful for students with autism. Teachers also need ongoing guidance and consultation from the inclusion coordinator, particularly when faced with complex issues that might arise during the day-to-day functioning of the classroom. In addition, training is necessary as new teachers are hired.

Inclusion Coordinator

Typically, the special education teacher functions as the coordinator since he or she is responsible for the implementation of Individualized Education Plan or Individual Education

Program (IEP) objectives, which are carried out within both special and regular education classes. This role can be assigned to a resource teacher, the school counselor, a lead teacher for special education, or an assistant vice principal. The role can be a time-intensive job and would be difficult for those who have other substantial duties in the school.

The primary responsibilities of the inclusion coordinator include program integration, training for the participating teachers, the provision of information and strategies that will be helpful in teaching a child with autism, participation in program evaluation, monitoring IEP objectives, etc. Therefore, the inclusion coordinator will need to be knowledgeable in such areas as instructional techniques that are useful with students with autism, positive behavioral programming, and social skills interventions. An inclusion coordinator is an added responsibility with additional duties that must be acknowledged by the school system.

Collaboration of Regular and Special Education

All teachers in the inclusion team must have the time to meet on a weekly or biweekly basis in order to evaluate the program, arrange appropriate scheduling for the students, problem-solve individual situations, and support each other in their efforts. A meeting including all participating teachers is a requirement of the EARC Inclusion Project and is advised for other schools attempting this style of programming. Though often difficult to obtain, teachers should try to have at least ten or fifteen minutes each morning with support personnel to coordinate the daily programming of the targeted child. This is important in order to ensure consistency and to make modifications in the child's curriculum. In addition, children with autism often require other services, such as speech and language therapy, occupational therapy, academic assistance, etc. In most instances, these services are most effectively delivered within the regular classroom setting. This enhances generalization. However, in some situations, individual or small group sessions may be necessary to offer more intensive interventions and reduce the stigma for the identified child. Regardless of the chosen service delivery model, the regular education teacher should have time to plan with the related services staff so that she or he is able to also work on those goals in the regular class.

Classroom Support

Special education support in the regular education classrooms will be necessary for paraprofessionals, aides, resource teachers, etc. The support will depend on the needs of the individual child. Full-time support is always ideal, but is not always necessary when considering an inclusion program for children with autism. Gains in social, linguistic, and academic functioning are not ensured by simply placing the child in a regular education setting. At least partial support of an aide or teacher is usually necessary for optimal academic and social progress. *This is often the determining factor for a successful inclusion program.*

IEP-Driven Program and Data Tracking

The best inclusion program is one that meets the student's IEP goals in the regular education environment. In order to evaluate progress of the program and assess whether IEP goals are being met, data must be taken periodically for analysis. In addition to monitoring IEP goals (which should include social goals), teachers should also monitor the student's use of appropriate social skills at the beginning, middle, and end of the school year. The initial database should include assessment of adaptive behaviors; for example, the *Vineland Adaptive Behavior Scale* measures social skills. Suggested assessments include *Walker-McConnell Scale of Social Competence and School Adjustment* by Singular Publishing Group, Inc.; *Walker Social Skills* by Pro-Ed; or *Skillstreaming* by Research Press); peer interviews; and teacher satisfaction. The teachers participating in the inclusion program will be expected to contribute to this effort throughout the year. Pre- and post-data should be taken, as well as periodic data on behaviors and social initiations throughout the school term.

Regular Education Ownership

Although this program is designed so that the regular education teacher receives lots of support (inclusion coordinator, special education teacher, paraprofessional, etc.), when it all comes down to it, the student is in his or her class. <u>Therefore, the teacher needs to take ownership for the student.</u> When a student is unable to participate in a full-day inclusion program, at least starting and ending the day in the regular education class will help the student feel like he or she is one of the class and not just a visitor. Also, counting the student with autism in the class numbers will help prevent the class from becoming overcrowded.

Collaboration between Home and School

Parents are a very important part of the inclusion projects. When the teachers and parents are able to work together as both educators and advocates for the student with autism, greater gains are usually seen. Collaboration between home and school helps the student with generalization of skills, as well as offers parents and teachers opportunities to exchange ideas about what strategies work best with the student.

References

Aloia, G., Beaver, R., & Pettus, W. (1978). Increasing initial interactions among integrate EMR students and their non-retarded peers in a game-playing situation. *American Journal of Mental Deficiency, 82,* 573-579.

Goldstein, H., & Ferrell, D. (1987). Augmenting communicative interaction between handicapped and non-handicapped preschool children. *Journal of Speech and Hearing Disorders*, 52, 200-211.

Goldstein, H., & Ferrell, D. (1987). Augmenting communicative interaction between handicapped and non-handicapped preschool children. *Journal of Speech and Hearing Disorders*, 52, 200-211.

Goldstein, H., Wiskstrom, S. (1986). Peer intervention effects on communicative interaction among handicapped and non-handicapped preschoolers. *Journal of Applied Behavior Analysis*, 19, 209-214.

Gresham, F., (1982). Misguided Mainstreaming: The Case for Social Skills Training with Handicapped Children. *Exceptional Children*, 48, Abstract.

Wooten, M., & Mesibov, G.B., (1986). Social Skills Training for Elementary School Autistic Children with Normal Peers. *Social Behavior in Autism*, edited by Schopler, E. and Mesibov, G.B., Plenum Publishing Corporation.

Inclusion Model

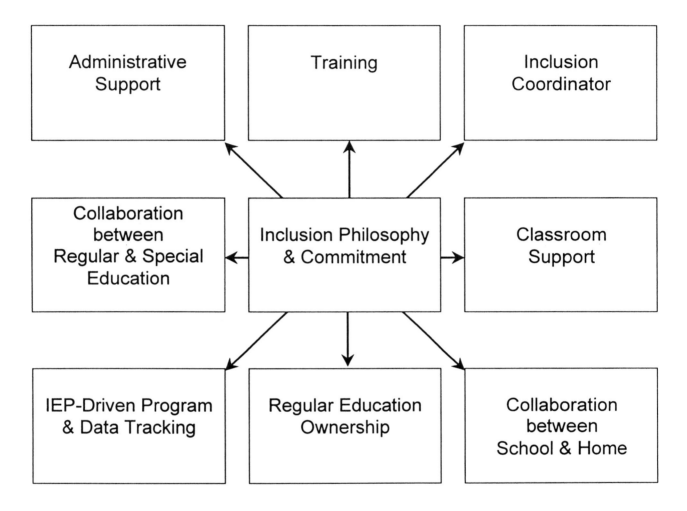

What is Autism?

Characteristics of Autism

Autism is a developmental disorder that is behaviorally defined. It is one of the five sub-categories of the pervasive developmental disorders as defined by the DSM-IV. Other sub-categories include Pervasive Developmental Disorder, not otherwise specified (PDD-NOS), Asperger Disorder, Rett Disorder, and Childhood Disintegrative Disorder. Although they range in severity and symptomatology, all of these disorders cause impairments in three categories: social, communication, and behavior. Below is a list of characteristics associated with autism.

Age of Onset/Development

- Deficits usually noted by three years of age
- Delay in onset of first words
- Delay in onset of first phrases
- Uneven skill development
- 60% have IQ's under 50; 20% have IQ's between 50-70; 20% have no mental retardation, with some individuals in the gifted range (these figures are only approximate)

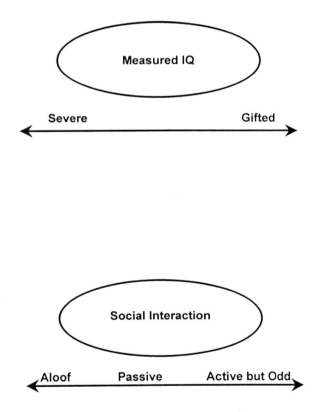

Social Domain

Impairments in:

- Understanding social gestures
- Eye contact
- Social smile (reciprocal)
- Showing and directing
- Sharing/turn-taking
- Offering/seeking comfort
- Appropriate use of facial expression
- Consistency of social responses
- Imaginative play

- Ability to play social games
- Ability to make friends
- Ability to judge social situations
- Imitative social play
- Interest in other children
- Response to other children
- Ability to "read" another's non-verbal cues

Communications Domain

Impairments in:

- Complexity of non-echoed utterances
- Functional language (often echolalic)
- Social "chat"
- Reciprocal conversation
- Appropriateness of language
    - Grammar/pronominal confusion
    - Use of neologisms
    - Idiosyncratic language
    - Demonstration of verbal rituals
- Imitation of language
- Pointing to express interest
- Instrumental gestures
- Nodding/head shaking, etc.
- Attention to voice modulation
- Comprehension of simple language
- Direct gaze
- Reciprocal gaze
- 40-45% of students with autism are nonverbal

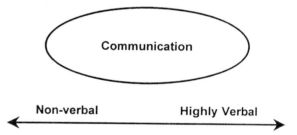

Behavioral Characteristics

Individuals with autism can have:

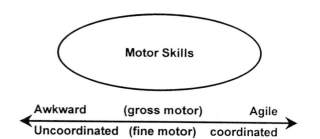

- Circumscribed interests
- Unusual preoccupations
- Repetitive use of objects
- Compulsions/rituals
- Unusual sensory interests
- Hand/finger mannerisms
- Other complex mannerisms, such as self-stimulatory behavior
- Self-injury
- Special skills

Miscellaneous Characteristics (Some statistics are subject to debate and need further research)

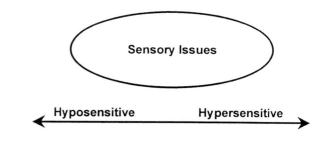

- 1/4 to 1/3 have epilepsy
- 4 out of 5 will be boys
- Girls usually have more severe characteristics
- Same incident rate in all countries, races, socio-economic status
- Some individuals have poor motor skills
- Some individuals have sensory issues

Individuals with autism can vary widely from one another. Although they may exhibit different characteristics among those outlined above, all individuals with autism have underlying similarities of impairment in communication, socialization, and in interests and behaviors. The severity range of autism can range from very mild to quite severely impaired. This can be confusing to many parents and professionals trying to understand the disorder of autism. However, parents and professionals need to remember that *all* individuals with autism can progress and learn when their programming is designed around their unique, specific needs.

Characteristics of Autism (1986; modified from Dalrymple, N.).

Characteristics of Asperger's Disorder

Asperger's Disorder (or Syndrome) is a relatively new diagnostic category in the DSM-IV under the umbrella of the pervasive developmental disorders. Until recently, individuals with Asperger's were often misdiagnosed as ADHD, schizophrenic, schizotypal personality disorder, learning disabled, etc. (or not diagnosed at all). More of these students are being identified and placed in regular education classrooms; however, most teachers and professionals are not familiar with this disorder. Asperger's Syndrome is very similar to high-functioning autism in many ways, and there is still some debate as to whether Asperger's Syndrome and high-functioning autism are indeed the same disorder, or whether Asperger's and Non-Verbal Learning Disorder is the same. The DSM-IV separates Asperger's Syndrome from autism by two diagnostic criteria: the child must have had typical language development and demonstrate normal to high cognitive ability. (It should be noted that some children with autism have average I.Q.'s as well). Children with Asperger's Syndrome are highly verbal, intelligent individuals who demonstrate impairments in reciprocal social interaction, communication (pragmatic language), and range of interests. They also often have motor difficulties, leading to an awkward gait and fine motor problems, although this certainly is not true in all individuals.

Common difficulties include

- Perseveration on specific topics of interest
- Insistence on sameness/difficulty with changes in routine
- Inability to make friends
- Difficulty with reciprocal conversations
- Pedantic speech
- Socially naive and literal thinkers
- Tend to be reclusive
- Difficulty with learning in large groups
- Difficulties with abstract concepts
- Problem-solving abilities tend to be poor
- Vocabulary usually great; comprehension poor
- Low frustration tolerance
- Poor coping strategies

- Restricted range of interests
- Poor writing skills (fine-motor problems)
- Poor concentration
- Academic difficulties
- Emotional vulnerability
- Poor organization skills
- Appear "normal" to other people
- Motor clumsiness

Because these children have so many strengths, it is often easy to overlook their weaknesses. Some of their behaviors may be interpreted as "spoiled" or "manipulative," and children with Asperger's are often considered defiant and "troublemakers."

It is important for teachers to recognize that inappropriate behaviors are usually a function of poor coping strategies, low frustration tolerance, and difficulty reading social cues. Most teaching strategies that are effective for students with autism (structure, consistency, etc.) also work for students with Asperger's. However, because these children are often aware that they are different and can be self-conscious about it, teachers may need to be subtler in their intervention methods.

Assessments

Reading - A
Math - A
Spelling - A
Writing - A

Great progress!

Programming for an Inclusive Setting:

Assessing the Individual Student

Each student placed in a regular education setting will have specific, individual needs that are different from any other student. There is no way to create an inclusive setting that will meet the needs of all children. However, there are strategies and methods that can increase the likelihood of the child experiencing success. Identifying the areas where the child may require help, and supporting the child and teacher with strategies and methods founded in research-based methods, can aid in creating a positive, inclusive environment. I hope the following suggestions will prove helpful to the teacher contemplating an inclusive program for students with autism. Many variables will interfere with this process, but it can be successful with proper planning and implementation.

Step One: Determine the strengths and weaknesses of the student

Academic

- Is the child on grade level?
- Does the child have adequate fine motor skills? What about pencil grips?
- Will the student need a modified curriculum, and if yes, in what?
- How long will the child attend?
- Does the student pick up verbal cues? (two- and three-step directions)
- Does the child have independent working skills?

Social Skills

- How does the child respond to other children?
- Can the student work closely with others?
- Does he or she share willingly?
- Does the child make eye contact with adults and children?
- Does he or she request help?
- Does the student initiate conversation with other children?
- Can he or she identify emotions in self or others?
- Does the child have appropriate play skills?

Behavioral

- How does the child express frustration?

- Can the child calm himself down?

- Is the child aggressive toward other children or adults?

- Can the child stay on task?

- How does the child handle free time?

- Can the child sit for extended periods of time?

- Does the child have disruptive behaviors?

- Will the child tolerate classroom noise?

Step Two: Observe the regular education classroom the child will attend

While in the classroom look for:

- Times the student will be independent and successful

- Times the student will need assistance

Step Three: Review IEP goals

- Determine how the goals can be taught in the classroom

- What areas will require additional help?

- What can be met within the natural activities of the day?

- Who will be responsible for each goal?

- What can be modeled by a peer? What must be taught one-on-one by the teacher?

Step Four: Determine the behavioral challenges the student will face

- Conduct a behavioral checklist.

- Determine what environmental changes are necessary to decrease problem behavior

- Is there a <u>behavior plan</u> already in operation?

- Determine natural consequences for when behavior does occur

- Decide who will implement the procedures:

  regular education teacher

  special education teacher

  regular education paraprofessional

  special education paraprofessional

  speech teacher, occupational therapist, or physical therapist

  related teacher: P.E., music, art, etc.

Step Five: Determine which social skills will be targeted in the classroom

- Run a social skills assessment

- Determine the long-term and short-term goals

- Determine the teaching methods you will use

  Large group, small group

  Games, puppets, role plays, rehearsal strategies

- Decide who will be responsible for monitoring the goals (see list above)

- Determine who will be responsible for tracking the generalization of objectives throughout the day.

Step Six: Conduct a reinforcer/motivational assessment

- Keep a running list of objects and activities that reinforce the student and give all members of team access to it.

- Periodically change the list as reinforcers change.

Step Seven: Set weekly or biweekly meetings with all people involved in the education of the student

- Set time for meeting during nap time, recess, snack, P.E., music, before or after school, or during video time

- Discuss successes, challenges, and what works and does not work

- Include parents in the meetings occasionally to get their opinions and ideas

Step Eight: Conclusions

- Can this child be immediately placed in regular education classes full-time?

- If not, what transition process is needed? What is the projected timeframe?

- How much paraprofessional support will be necessary to sustain this child successfully?

- How quickly can the support be faded?

- How much partial support will be needed on a permanent basis?

- What is the bare minimum that will be needed to ensure success?

A successful inclusion program will face many challenges, often from sources other than that which the individual student with autism presents. Special education teachers must continually assess the inclusive setting for possible saboteurs. They must remain flexible and willing to cooperate with a variety of people in the school's administration. Also, enthusiasm must not waver, even in the face of disappointment, for many people will look to the teacher to provide the resources and encouragement that they will need for the inclusion program. Students with autism deserve the opportunity to have exposure to typical students in their schools. Careful planning and implementation will ensure the success of the program and be an encouragement for others to follow in their footsteps.

Assessing the School, Teachers, and Classroom

Teachers often begin the process of inclusion by seeking information regarding the best methods and strategies available for designing a successful program for their students. However, too often, these same teachers are met with frustration and confusion when they are unable to find methods that can readily lend themselves to the implementation of a consistent program. I hope that the following suggestions will prove helpful to teachers when they consider assessing their school and classrooms for inclusion programs for their students.

Innumerable variables can affect any inclusion program, and the wise teacher will assess not only the potential students, but also the school, teachers, and classrooms. The list of components may seem daunting at first, but with proper preparation and flexibility, an inclusion program can succeed.

Step One: Assess the school

- How accepting is your school of students with disabilities?

- Are there other students with disabilities in inclusive programs?

- Does your principal welcome this suggestion? How will the principal respond if parents call to discuss problem situations?

- Is your principal a micro-manager or macro-manager?

- Will the principal be able to offer concrete support and advice, or just moral support?

- Do you have a school counselor? How effective is she or he?

- Does the counselor conduct social skills groups with any students?

- Are parents in your area generally accepting of individuals with disabilities? Is there a support network?

- Do the regular education teachers seem receptive to an inclusive program? What do these teachers say in the breakroom?

- Does your school have established peer tutor programs? How effective are they? Are they formal or informal? If you currently do not have peer tutor programs, is the school open to setting them up?

Step Two: Special education teacher assessment

- Will you be required to retain your classroom and students?

- How many students are on your caseload?

- If you have a classroom of students **not** included, how much time can you devote in the regular education class?

- Will your paraprofessionals be pulled from the inclusion project for other job duties? (bus, lunch, coverage of absent staff, etc.).

- Do the teachers understand that your students will be counted in the total number of regular education students per class?

- How many students do you project putting in regular education?

- Do you have enough staff for adequate support?

- Do you have students that can share support?

- Will the school allow time for the participating teachers to meet before or after school? What about including the paraprofessionals and aides?

- Will the school provide substitutes so that you can offer training sessions to all teachers participating in the project?

- Will you be able to "float" among the classrooms, or will you have your own class load?

- Will you be team-teaching?

- Can you provide modified academic support to your students, or will you have to have the regular education teacher do this? Do you have all the materials you need?

- Do you have a good relationship with the regular education teacher?

- How diplomatic are you at approaching problems with regular education teachers? Can you maintain your professionalism when stressed?

- Do you understand the importance of eating lunch with the regular education teachers and your support staff?

Step Three: Regular education teacher assessment

- What is the teacher's style of teaching? Small group or large group?

- How does the teacher handle behavior problems? Is he or she just targeting the negative behaviors? Is the teacher running a response cost system?

- How are the desks arranged (rows, groupings, etc.)?

- Is this a structured teacher? Does her or his daily schedule stay the same, or are there continual changes from day-to-day?

- Is the teacher warm and nurturing?

- Is the teacher a strict disciplinarian?

- Is he or she flexible?

- Will the teacher allow you to co-teach?

- Will he or she be bothered by other adults in the room?

- Will the teacher accept taking data occasionally?

- Does the teacher use many manipulatives?

- Does he or she allow times for social gatherings?

- Will the teacher allow you to pull a few students for social games or peer programs? If not, what about recess?

- Will he or she claim the student as his or her own?

- Will the teacher let you conduct disability awareness classes?

- Will he or she allow peer programs to be conducted?

- How consistent is he or she in methods?

- Is the teacher willing to teach your student?

- Does she or he teach through positive methods? (Take a baseline of how many positive contacts the teacher has versus negative contacts with students for thirty or sixty minutes.)

- Does the teacher have a classroom aide? How does she or he view their job duties?

- Does your teacher seem happy in the job or burned-out?

- Are all the students treated fairly? Are there teacher's pets? What about troublemakers?

Step Four: Support personnel assessment

- How is your support person funded? Is he or she a regular education paraprofessional/aide, or a special education paraprofessional/aide?

- How does the aide understand the job duties if he or she is a regular education aide?

- How competent is this person? Can she or he be relied upon to actually teach?

- What does the aide do during down time? Does the aide take the initiative to plan additional activities, or does she or he need continual direction?

- Can the aide handle problem behaviors in a positive manner?

- Is the aide afraid of our students?

- How often does he or she use negatives with students?

- Does the aide have problem-solving abilities?

- Can he or she get along well with the regular education teachers?

- Can the aide work in the regular education class with minimal distraction to the overall lessons going on?

- Does the aide seem to like working with the children? Does she or he play favorites? Is any child slighted?

- Can the aide be creative? Can he or she change tactics easily?

- How independent is the aide? Can he or she do academic modification?

Step Five: Classroom assessment

- How many children are in the classroom?

- Have they reached maximum numbers, or do you project that more will be added?

- Are there good role models for social development?

- What are the traffic patterns like?

- Are the students seated in individual desks or at tables?

- Where would your student sit in the existing arrangement?

- Can students share materials easily?

- Will your student be facing a door or a window?

- Is the schedule posted for all to see easily?

- Are children identified by names on name tags, chairs, etc.?

- How do the students progress from the room to other rooms?

- Where do the students sit during lunch? Is there room for your student(s)?

- Are there any bullies in the room?

- Is there a bathroom nearby?

- How will you handle inappropriate behavior in this classroom?

- Is there a quiet corner?

- Is this a noisy classroom? How will your student handle it if it is?

Step Six: Parent assessment

- How involved are the student's parents?

- Do they have the potential to "burn out" teachers?

- Are your parents willing to have periodic meetings?

- Would they agree to parent training sessions to aid in the generalization of skills?

- Would the parents be available as parent-volunteers in the classroom?

- How consistent is the follow-through in the home setting?

- What are the expectations of the parents?

- Are they realistic of **your** potential and their child's?

- How supportive are they of you and the regular education teacher?

I hope these suggestions will provide the beginning questions that teachers must ask before conducting an inclusion program for students with autism. There are, most likely, many more that you will be able to consider for your own particular school, teacher, support, etc.

A Principal's Role in Inclusion

The principal's role in inclusion is one of the major components that makes up a good program. Teachers cannot do all that is necessary without the input, supervision, support, understanding, and collaboration of the principal. Also, the longevity of the program will depend on how much the principal believes in the project. If he or she only gives lip service to the teachers and training staff, the teachers begin to feel that they are out on a limb, and they suffer all of the traditional woes of unsupported teachers. The principal needs to feel that he or she is part of the team that is conducting inclusion. He or she must welcome any participation on any level. The principal should consider the following issues when establishing an inclusion program.

Staff Roles

Teachers who are involved with inclusion are taking on new roles in the school. The teachers' workloads will be much heavier and more intense as they work to carry out the program to educate the student with autism in their classroom. Many times, teachers become so overloaded that their stress levels skyrocket. They need the principal's understanding when he or she assigns other school-related duties to them. If possible, the principal should go light on the teachers the year that they have someone with autism in their class. Also, if there is an inclusion coordinator, she or he will have a very delicate role to play. The coordinator must be able to work with both special and regular education teachers and help them mesh together. The coordinator will be on their "turf", so to speak, which can cause problems. The inclusion coordinator must have the principal's backing and full support for what they are doing. Many times, inclusion coordinators feel as if they do not belong anywhere and are set out to drift, so it is important for the principal to take ownership of them immediately and offer support.

The role of the paraprofessional is also one that is crucial to this project. Schools use paraprofessionals in a number of roles; e.g., giving out medication, doing bus duty, copying materials, running errands, etc. However, whenever a paraprofessional is pulled from the student she or he is assigned to help, major disruptions can occur with that student and classroom. Some of the most difficult times have come because the paraprofessional has been pulled by the administration to perform a job that is not part of her or his role as a special education paraprofessional to the program. Students with autism have major problems with transitions and changes. Changes and transitions usually present teachers with "wonderful" new behaviors (!) that can also affect people outside the classroom. If possible, limit the times that the paraprofessionals are pulled from their duties with the students.

Chain of Command

The model for the chain of command in the school is important. Teachers and paraprofessionals need to understand that there is a hierarchy for accomplishing tasks. All personnel in an inclusion project must adhere to school policies. For example, teachers (not the paraprofessionals) must make phone calls to parents, and the teachers need to sign the daily journals. Often people make decisions without understanding that they cannot do that particular action. For example: a paraprofessional pulling a student out of his regular education class to participate in another class for one special activity, thus missing the activities in his own class. Although the student may wish to participate, the guidelines of the IEP do not allow it. Teachers must understand that the IEP is a legal document, and they can place themselves at risk of a lawsuit if the IEP is not followed to the letter. Most teachers do not truly understand this. It is the job of the principal to inform them.

Teacher Selection

Whereas volunteers for inclusion teacher positions are ideal, this is not always possible. Teachers must understand that the principal will place students with autism into classrooms, even if a teacher does not want them there. Unfortunately, a choice is not always possible or given. The principal may receive flak for this, but in essence, the teacher has the ultimate choice of teaching in the school or not. Students with autism do not have a choice as to whether they have autism or not. However, the principal should try **very hard** to win teachers over and have them enjoy their year with an inclusion project. After all, it is better to work and learn from a happy teacher than an unhappy one!

Each spring, new teachers will be solicited for the students moving up a grade. The inclusion coordinator should have input into the decisions as to which class the students will be placed. Also, please consider choosing teachers early enough so that the new teacher can go into the class and observe the new student. This probably means some release time in the spring. Planning early for this activity, so that budgets will allow for it, is always advisable. Smooth transitions between school years can make a world of difference for both teachers and students, and in resulting behaviors. When choosing a teacher, remember that structured, yet flexible, teachers work best for an inclusion project. Strict disciplinarians, who cannot adjust to new situations and new problems, have not done well at all in our project. A nurturing quality on the part of the teacher helps immensely.

Substitutes

It can be very difficult to obtain the exact number of substitutes needed when teachers or assistants are out because of illness. However, when a staff member working with a student with autism is out, it can have **tremendous** ramifications. If at all possible, please make sure that a substitute teacher or paraprofessional is available for the student when a member of the inclusion team is home ill.

Working with Parents

The parents and the school should work together as a collaborative team. Many parents of students in inclusion projects have become the school's strongest supporters. Many times, however, parents of inclusion students who are not as strongly supported can become overly focused on the program, leading to tremendous conflicts between home and school. Boundaries often get crossed, leading to teacher, administration, and parent burn-out. It helps greatly if the school has set visitor policies that are strictly enforced. Some parents have been known to wander all over the school looking into each classroom, disrupting activities and lessons, while they look for a member of the inclusion team. Also, overly frequent contact between the inclusion coordinator or teachers and the parents (especially calls at night) can lead to burn-out, causing some teachers to quit their jobs.

Parents are wonderful people who are justified in seeing that their child is obtaining the best education possible. Nevertheless, they sometimes do not understand the boundaries between school and home and can cause major problems when the principal does not structure the visits or provide the parents concrete directions regarding visits to the school. Conversely, teachers can never fully appreciate what parents go through living with a child who happens to have autism. Some teachers may make disparaging remarks regarding parenting skills, attention, etc., which are usually untrue and are best left unsaid. Again, the principal must serve as a role model for both teachers and parents in how to form and continue relationships between the home and school environments.

Philosophy

The principal sets the philosophy of the school. He or she is the role model for the teachers. That a principal has chosen to allow inclusion in the school says a lot about her or him as a person. This will help the whole school staff embrace this new change and make it something to be proud of.

Much of the philosophy will come from the principal. The teachers will readily embrace the principal's views when they see that he or she is a strong believer in this style of teaching. Entire schools can change dramatically when the principal leads the way to best practices, and it can be thrilling to watch the changes occur.

Visitors to the Program

Many people and schools will be interested in a well-run inclusion project. Although it is exciting to "spread the news," there are some cautionary notes. Visitors are discouraged for the first two to three months of a program to allow people to adjust to the changes, the students to get used to the school and their classrooms, and for the teachers to feel comfortable. After this time, small groups of people can come to learn about the program and talk to the staff. This can become oppressive if too many people come at once, so setting one day per month for visitors, and limiting the numbers that come into the classroom at one time, is a good idea.

Suspension from School

Schools must follow the regulations regarding suspension from school for specified actions.* However, students with autism often show aggression toward other people as a result of their disability. The principal should be assured that this is an area that inclusion teachers target specifically for extinction and that flexibility in this matter is greatly appreciated.

Creating a Win-Win IEP by Future Horizons, Arlington, Texas, covers this issue very well.

How Do We Impact
Social Skills?

Social Skills for Children with Autism

A Regular Education Experience

Children with autism have much to gain from typical children in regular education. We look to regular education to provide the social and communication role models that children with autism require. We place children with autism in the regular education setting because peers are the best models of typical behavior. The peers demonstrate how to play with another child, how to share, how to take turns, how to gesture, how to use facial expression, how to ask for help, how to play a particular game, etc. The lessons that children with autism learn from their typical classmates are invaluable.

When placing children with autism within regular education, appropriate social behaviors need to be identified for their particular classroom, as they do with all children. Teachers often have their own classroom rules for acceptable social and academic behavior. Many children with autism do not understand what is socially appropriate and what is inappropriate. Therefore, they will need to be taught the accepted behaviors. Their inappropriate behaviors may discourage other children from playing or interacting with them, as well as cause disruptions in the classroom. For example, many children with autism prefer to play alone. They may wander away from a group or refuse to take their turn because they do not understand the rules of the activity. Having exposure to typical children can help to teach these children how to play the group activity and how to share materials or turns. Another example is when children need help with an activity. Instead of raising their hands to gain the teacher's attention, they may get up and get the needed materials themselves (disrupting the class), or they may interrupt classroom instruction by verbally requesting what they need.

In the same way that we give extra help to a student who is having trouble in math, we need to understand and help those who are having trouble using or understanding social skills. Because of the deficits in the social domain, children with autism do need this help; they do not usually learn these behaviors on their own.

Social skills, as defined in the *Walker Social Skills Curriculum* (Pro-Ed), are skills that:

- allow for proper initiations toward others, as well as maintain positive relationships with others

- allow for peer acceptance in the classroom, work place, and community

- enable one to cope and adapt to the social environment

A child may lack social skills for several reasons:

- He or she does not understand social cues from the environment

  For example: the child cannot tell when a person is not interested in what he or she is talking about, or the child cannot initiate play with another child because he or she cannot make eye contact

- The child does not know the appropriate way to respond to the environment

- He or she does not practice the skill enough to use it naturally

- The child cannot control emotions enough to think about an appropriate response.

The lack of social skills often exhibits itself in ways we do not attribute to a social deficit.

For example:

Yelling or calling out inappropriate statements at inappropriate times

If typical children want attention, they know to approach someone and initiate contact by showing them something, telling them something, etc. A child with autism may not have this means of communication to initiate in the same way as the non-disabled child.

Aggression/destruction

Typical children learn they can negotiate, talk about, or come up with a solution to solve a problem they may have. Children with autism may not have the problem-solving skills or the language skills to communicate what they need. Instead, they might exhibit aggression toward someone else to gain the needed attention.

Echolalia/Jargon

Sometimes children with autism do not know or understand which words would be appropriate to the context, with the result that they use the only words they do know or are capable of speaking. This may be in the form of echolalia or jargon (nonsense words). Teachers and parents need to teach appropriate words to say so that the children will be able to communicate appropriately.

Inappropriate touching of others

Without appropriate means of getting attention, children sometimes use touch too roughly, may touch others in sensitive places, or embarrass another child by their actions. Teachers and peers may be called upon to teach the child with autism the correct way to touch others through modeling and physical assistance. The child will learn best when this teaching is done immediately after the inappropriate touching.

Avoidance

Many children with autism prefer to be alone, instead of interacting with their peers. While this does not usually cause a disruption to the regular education classroom, the children are not learning much needed social skills and this prevents them from forming friendships.

Teachers should view inappropriate behaviors as excellent opportunities for teaching. Whenever an inappropriate behavior occurs, the teacher then has an opportunity to intervene immediately and teach the correct skill. Viewing inappropriate behaviors as teaching units, rather than as disruptions, will aid the child with autism and improve the teacher's effectiveness with the child. A teaching contact is any situation used to foster the growth of social skills. Every initiation a child makes can be turned into a teaching contact. Teaching contacts are:

Redirection of inappropriate initiations

This includes interrupting the inappropriate behavior, describing or modeling the desired response, and having the student use the more appropriate response immediately.

Praising of appropriate interactions

The student needs to learn that using an appropriate interaction strategy can get the desired response. Therefore, when the student tries the new strategy, he she should receive praise, rewards, and the desired response. It is important to continuing reinforcing this new behavior so that it remains in the student's repertoire of social strategies. This means catching the student when using appropriate strategies and reinforcing those strategies with praise and rewards.

For example:

>Johnny wants a crayon.
>Billy has it.
>Johnny grabs the crayon from Billy.

The teaching contact would be a redirection to the correct way to get the crayon, versus a punishment like yelling, " Stop that," or "Give him back his crayon."

For example:

> Johnny grabs the crayon from Billy.
> Teacher says, " Johnny, do you want a crayon?" or "What do you do if you want a crayon?"
> Johnny does nothing.
> Teacher says, "You can ask Billy for that crayon," or "When Billy is done you may ask for the crayon."

In this case, Johnny demonstrates his lack of the appropriate behavior necessary to gain the crayon. Teachers must understand that Johnny does not understand the appropriate behavior and cannot be held responsible for a skill until it is learned. The teacher then uses that situation to teach him the correct method of gaining it.

If the environment is set up to promote peer interactions, meeting these goals can become a natural part of the classroom environment. Opportunities for natural social interaction increase when the target student is seated next to peers and activities are designed for students to work on in small groups or pairs. It is also important that the activities provide ample opportunity for language, and all students are encouraged to help before asking for the teacher's assistance ("Ask three before me"). The teacher must create a positive and cooperative atmosphere in the classroom.

There are also specific ways to teach social skills. Within the classroom, a social skills element can be added to the curriculum and taught to the entire class by using puppets, games, or role play situations. Typical children often need to learn social skills as much as the target child. There are several different ways to teach social skills in a structured manner. This book contains in-depth descriptions of the methods mentioned below.

Social skills instruction and class-wide reinforcement

Social skills can be taught class-wide or on a smaller scale with just a few children. The group of students should always include more typical children than target children to promote modeling of age-appropriate behavior. The goal of a social skills lesson is to use direct instruction to teach children targeted social skills and what to say and do in certain social situations. Role plays, games, and simple incidental teaching can be used during the group time to give the children every opportunity to practice the skills being taught. Class-wide reinforcement systems can be used to help encourage students to practice targeted social skills throughout the day.

Friends Club

A Friends Club is a group of students who agree to take turns playing with the target child at recess, center time, or during times when partners are needed. All volunteers' names are put into a jar. One to two names are drawn from the jar, and those students spend the designated time with the target child. These students are educated about what to expect from the target child, how to handle situations that come up, and are given plenty of praise and support for their efforts.

Peer Tutoring

Peer tutors can be participants of the Friends Club or can be chosen from the class as needed. A peer tutor will work one-on-one to aid with academics, social skills, or classroom activities as needed by the target child. The peer stays with the child during typically difficult times for the child, or designated times of the day, and works on specific areas of need. It works well to pull a peer tutor for a target child as a way to prevent minor disruptive or inappropriate behavior; e.g., dealing with transitions, walking in line, being quiet in the halls, etc.

The Lunch Bunch

As used by Mt. Bethel Elementary School, *The Lunch Bunch* is an excellent method to teach social skills using a small group of typical peers during lunch. The student with autism chooses three or four peers to eat lunch with him or her in a quiet place and work on conversation and social skills in a teacher-facilitated group. (Please see the chapter outlining the Lunch Bunch.)

Social Games

Any game can be made into a social game by encouraging social goals that are needed by the target student. The use of games is a fun way to encourage social skills among children. Also, games that incorporate objects or activities that are highly reinforcing to a socially isolated student can increase his or her motivation for social interaction with peers.

Rehearsal Strategies

A rehearsal strategy is a way to go over social rules in certain situations prior to that situation occurring. It is a way to remind the child how to act, what to say, or what to do in situations the child may have had trouble with in the past. Rehearsal strategies can include short stories such as Carol Gray's *Social Stories*, that talk about a topic of concern for the child. In *Social Stories*, as defined by Carol Gray, the sentences should be written in first person (from the child's perspective) and describe where the situation occurs, who is involved, what is happening and why. The students can then be given the story to read at the beginning and end of the day, so that when the situation comes up, they have read about it and understand what is expected.

Being a part of regular education is a critical component of the target child's social development. With the proper guidance, the student can become an active participant in the regular education class. As social skills are encouraged in the target child, all children benefit. The students in the class learn to accept and assist their classmates with special needs, forming more positive relationships for the future.

References

Skillstreaming, (Research Press Co., 2612 N. Mattis Ave., Champaign, Illinois)

Gray, C. (1993), *The Original Story Book*, (Future Horizons, Inc., Arlington, Texas)

Gray, C. (1994), *The New Social Story Book*, (Future Horizons, Inc., Arlington, Texas)

Walker Social Skills Curriculum, (Pro-Ed, 8700 Shoal Creek Blvd, Austin, Texas)

Training Typical Peers for Social Intervention

Although access to typical peers is the goal of inclusion, many regular education teachers struggle with how to explain the student's needs and difficulties to the other students. Many typical students notice the differences between themselves and the student with autism in their class, but accept them anyway. However, this often does not happen automatically. Luckily, with proper training and information, typical students can learn to not only to accept these students as their friends, but also how to help the target student with learning new social behaviors.

Although we rarely identify the particular disorder of autism to the general education elementary students, if you find it necessary to do so, then you must ask permission from the parents before identifying the target child. Some parents of children with autism do not like to have their child's disability announced to the entire class or have the child acknowledged as someone who is "different" from the other children. Because this is a sensitive issue for some parents, it is wise to discuss your program with the target child's parents before proceeding further.

If the parents are not comfortable with having their child identified as "different," the teacher can conduct the lesson with the entire class present and refrain from mentioning any details about the target student. This would impact the target child, maintain anonymity, and most likely benefit the typical children as well.

Training the entire classroom should be conducted, initially, when the target child is not in the room. The teacher should not go into precise details about the definition of autism unless needed. He or she should, however, stress the following points:

All children are different from one another

- Some children have brown hair, some black, some blonde, some red, etc.
- Some children need eye glasses, some do not
- Some children read very well, some do not
- Some children need help from others to figure out math problems; some are great at math
- Some children seem to make friends easily; some do not
- Some kids need help to know how to play or act; others don't

All children are the same in many ways, too

- All smile, all cry, all communicate in some fashion

- All have someone to take care of them

All children are different and yet the same. If all children were the same, it would be a very boring world!

Children with disabilities may seem different in some ways, but they are alike in more ways than they are different

The teacher can let the children discuss ways in which they are the same or different. Children can come up with some unusual statements or concepts of similarities or dissimilarities, which should be listened to very carefully and corrected, if necessary. Teachers can obtain some idea of the typical child's impressions and knowledge of disabilities in this manner.

After they have had this initial discussion, the teacher should give basic information on the specific difficulties the target child has, such as communication difficulties, social difficulties, and short descriptions of some of the unusual behaviors. Inform the children that none of the behaviors are "contagious" and that they will not become "different" by playing with the child. This may help to alleviate some fears that typical children can sometimes have for children with disabilities.

The teacher should then have the students discuss ways they can help the target student throughout the day. The teacher should help lead the students to appropriate helping strategies and correct any inappropriate responses. For example:

- What could you do if you saw _____(target child) playing alone at recess?

- What could you do if _____(target child) was talking loudly during story time?

- What could you say if _____(target child) hugged you too hard?

- If _____(target child) wanted a toy you were playing with, how could you help him learn how to ask for it?

In the early grades (K-3rd), children usually accept students with disabilities and offer help without needing information on their particular diagnosis. However, older students are often less accepting of students' differences and less willing to help when they do not understand the reasons behind the disability. Therefore, for upper classrooms, the teacher may wish to talk more specifically about autism and explain why the target student has certain difficulties. The teacher should judge the maturity level of the students and tailor the discussion to meet their comprehension ability.

Classroom Social Skills Lessons

Social skills are usually not a part of the regular education curriculum. However, teaching social skills in the classroom can truly benefit students with autism and their typical peers.

Students with autism are often placed in regular education classrooms to learn social skills from their typical peers. Therefore, it is important that the regular education students are able to model appropriate social skills themselves. Teaching students appropriate social skills as a class helps mold the students into a more cohesive group and provides them opportunities to work together on positive role-modeling. Also, when an entire class is working on a particular skill at once, the student with autism can see many examples of others demonstrating that skill and have many opportunities to practice it in a short period of time. For a student for whom social skills do not come naturally, this type of direct instruction can be very beneficial.

Numerous social skills curricula are available to guide teachers on appropriate objectives to target with particular students. Indeed, many have their own rating forms, making it easy to identify particular areas of weakness for an individual student. Teachers can use a social skills curriculum like the *Walker Social Skills Curriculum* (Pro-Ed), *Walker-McConnell Scale of Social Competence and School Adjustment* (Singular Publishing Group, Inc.), or *Skillstreaming* (Research Press) to guide their instruction. These curricula offer comprehensive outlines of appropriate social skills used at school. (We suggest that these forms also be completed by the parents to provide additional information).

Social skills lessons are best presented early each Monday. These lessons usually take ten or fifteen minutes. The skills can be presented in a variety of ways: reading books on the subject, having a puppet show, guiding a classroom discussion, role playing a situation, rehearsing a script, playing games, etc. Once the skill lesson has been completed, the teacher should then encourage the students to try to use this skill throughout the week as often as possible. Throughout the course of the week, the teacher should target this skill for incidental teaching techniques.

The teacher can then conduct a meeting every Friday for ten or fifteen minutes near the end of the day, to allow the students to explain how they used the skill during the week. This provides an opportunity for the children, in a guided discussion, to talk about using this skill and how it helped them to interact with each other. At this point, the teacher should provide praise, and possibly reinforcement, to the students for their hard work.

To keep the students' level of motivation high for using each of the targeted skills, a class-wide positive reinforcement system can be included. This system can work in conjunction with the *Marble Ja*r (see the following discussion) At the end of each day, the teacher should announce which student used the targeted social skill the best throughout the day. That student can then receive a marble for the class. The "Social Skills Marble" should be a different color from the marbles used for the *Marble Jar*, but it should be added to the jar and count toward the fifty to one hundred marble goal to receive the class-wide reward. Therefore, each day, two or three regular marbles (as per *Marble Jar* program) and one social skills marble will be added to the *Marble Jar*, increasing the level of excitement and motivation for the program.

The Modified Marble Jar

A Class-Wide Peer Reinforcement System for Inclusive Settings[1]

Students with special needs who are currently placed in inclusive settings too often continue to experience isolation, despite being surrounded by strong social and language models. As is the case with children with autism, proximity is generally insufficient to assimilate and spontaneously demonstrate the needed social skills. In addition, opinions of the typical students towards the special needs child often become negative because they receive limited guidance on how to interact with the child with a handicap, and when they do approach and gain a positive response, they receive no reinforcement or encouragement for their efforts.

Special education teachers and parents often view regular education exposure for the child or student with trepidation because they feel the child will be ridiculed and teased by the other students. However, through formal peer tutoring programs, which elicit the support and assistance of all of the students, children with special needs will have multiple opportunities for positive interactions with their typical classmates. As a result, this can lead to the development of appropriate social behaviors for all students.

The *Modified Marble Jar* program is a class-wide reinforcement system (based on *Marbles in a Jar*, Canter, L.) used to encourage all students in a regular education classroom to spontaneously and positively interact with each other. Through an intermittent reinforcement schedule, the students begin to recognize the need for assistance in each other, and eventually respond without needing coaching or cues from the teachers or aides. Children with special needs placed in inclusive settings typically present multiple opportunities of need, thereby eliciting numerous social bids through the presentation of assistance from their peers, which is then intermittently reinforced by the class-wide reinforcement program.

Children with autism demonstrate significant social and language impairments. They typically have difficulty time-relating and interacting with others, especially with their age-mates in schools. In order for the child with autism to learn the needed social skills, he or she must first have numerous, and daily, positive social contacts to which he or she must react. Subsequently, it takes initiations by peers to provide these interactions. Through a Friends Club or a peer buddy system, the child with autism is exposed to many different social interactions and relationships. Often, due to the lack of social reciprocity, typical

---

[1] Presented at Association For Behavior Analysis, 1997

peers can become tired and discouraged when trying to initiate play. In an effort to address this "peer burn-out", the *Marble Jar* was developed and implemented in the EARC Inclusion Project. This program is an excellent way to keep all the children motivated to help each other, play with each other, and learn from each other.

The first step is to introduce the *Marble Jar* to the class (one jar per class). You should tell the students that this is a team effort where everyone will work together. Tell the students that the *Marble Jar* can help remind the students of how they can be a team. One marble is placed in the jar whenever the teacher notices a student helping another student who is having difficulty (without being told to help), a student being a friend to someone, a child being nice to a neighbor, or a child practicing the social skills lesson during the day.

This procedure continues until the classroom jar receives a designated number of marbles (between fifty and one hundred), and the entire class is then rewarded. Fifty marbles has proven to be ideal in many classes because the students perceive the number to be more attainable in the near future.

To maintain the enthusiasm, two or three marbles should be rewarded each day. The students responsible for the class receiving each marble should be congratulated and praised in front of the entire class (immediately after receiving the award, if possible). The classroom reinforcement for obtaining the desired amount should be a highly motivating activity; e.g., a class party or event. This is an excellent method for obtaining parental involvement because many parents enjoy preparing treats, supplying materials or activities for the classroom party, etc. The classroom students debate the reinforcement and make the final decision. The wise teacher will only **guide** the selection of the reinforcement and then heed the class selection of it in order to fully empower the program. Once the party is over, the jar is emptied and the process begins again.

Note: A marble is **never** taken out of the jar for misbehavior. The students should know that once they earn a marble, it will never be taken away for misbehavior.

Suggestions for ways to use the *Marble Jar* program

Social skills instruction

Individual objectives can be addressed by reinforcement of spontaneous demonstration of a social skill. For example, the teacher notices two children taking turns at the computer. The teacher announces, "I see John and Beth taking turns on the computer. That is a skill we are learning, and I am going to put one marble in the jar. Congratulations!"

The teacher observes as a child asks a classmate with a disability to play during recess. The teacher praises the child and announces to the class that they get another marble in the jar for asking one of the classmates to play. Without being asked, a child helps his or her friend pick up the crayons that fell. The teacher notices this kind action and tells the student to put a marble in the marble jar for being nice and helping a friend.

Behavior Management

Lee Canter's *Marbles in a Jar* program (assertive discipline) uses this style of reinforcement for encouraging replacement behaviors and for behavior reinforcement. However, the goal of the *Marble Jar* program is to encourage and increase interactions between disabled and non-disabled students. As such, this program strictly targets social skills, rather than calling attention to, or decreasing the rate and frequency of, an individual student's inappropriate behaviors. This program should be used for a social emphasis targeting the students' helping and befriending one another. It should not be based solely on following classroom "rules." This is an important difference!

The *Marble Jar* has been implemented on a daily basis in the EARC Inclusion Project. For example, in one classroom, the regular education teacher has two children with autism and nineteen other students. The first few weeks were difficult for the teacher to adapt her classroom to all the needs of her students. After one month, the *Marble Jar* program was introduced, and the teacher began implementation. Due to the program's impact on both the teacher and students, the classroom became an overwhelmingly positive environment for both disabled and non-disabled students. The amount of positive praise and encouragement resulted in increases in social bids toward the disabled children, increases in IEP social gains, and increases in the typical students' awareness and extreme sensitivity to helping one another throughout the day, eliminating many instances of teacher direction or redirection.

The *Marble Jar* program enabled this teacher, as well as many other teachers, to develop strong, positive environments that are rich in social opportunities for all students. As a result, inclusive classrooms become welcoming environments that teach social skills, and the benefits to disabled students and their typical classmates are immeasurable.

Reference

Canter, L., (1987). Assertive Discipline. Lee Canter & Associates, CA.

The Friends Club

A Friends Club is a positive way to encourage social skills in a child with autism. In general, children with autism prefer to play alone rather than to seek out and interact with peers. Therefore, teachers often have to "set up" situations that encourage appropriate play, as well as to develop the student's interest in playing with his or her peers. A Friends Club gives the child with autism exposure to peer interactions and gives the peers the opportunity to get to know the target child as a contributing member of their class.

A Friends Club is a group of student volunteers who agree to take turns playing with the target child during designated times. Through play, the peer buddy models typical social behavior in its naturally occurring setting. The target child best learns appropriate social behavior when demonstrated in the setting in which it is used. As the children begin to have fun, playing with each other becomes a desired activity. Students see that peer interaction is a positive experience, and the target child has an opportunity to see how social behavior should be used. The following steps are offered to schools as a method to organize and conduct the Friends Club.

Step One: Explain the situation

During a time when the target child is not in the room, explain to the children who have volunteered for the Friends Club about their own similarities and differences. Point out that they all have a body; however, they have different hair color, different interests, different needs, and so on. They are happy sometimes and sad other times. Children are the same in some ways and different in other ways, and this is OK. Without differences, the world would be a very boring place!

Tell the children that in order to help each other, we all have to make provisions for our differences. Just like when children need help in math, someone who understands math must show them how to do it. It is the same for a child who does not know how to play. Someone who **does** know how to play needs to teach the child how.

Once the children understand this, they need to understand the differences and similarities of children with autism. Language delays, social problems, and unusual habits or routines all need to be explained so the peer buddies will know what to expect while playing with the target child. It is not necessary to get too technical about the disorder. Be sure to include things the students will have in common with the child with autism in order to encourage a positive opinion of that child.

The children should have the opportunity to discuss their thoughts and feelings with the group. This is a good time for the teacher to notice any opinions or misunderstandings the children may have about being a part of the Friends Club.

Step Two: Explain what the Friends Club is and what the students will do

Students will put their names in a jar on a slip of paper. At the start of recess, group projects, games involving partners, etc., one or two student names will be drawn from the jar. The names drawn from the jar will be the target child's peer buddies for the designated activity. During recess, a buddy will play with the target child for five or ten minutes at the beginning of the recess period and five or ten minutes at the end of the recess period.

During a project or game, the buddy will be the target child's partner as long as the target child is willing to participate. After a name is drawn, it is put into a separate jar until everyone has had a turn. Once everyone has had a turn, the names are put back into the first jar and the process begins again.

When explaining the program, you should do it in a way that sounds fun and rewarding. Pulling the names out of a jar creates an element of surprise that is fun for the students. The jar should be decorated in bright colors to help create interest. Another way to foster interest among the children who volunteer for the Friends Club is to allow them to decorate their own name tags to be drawn out of the jar. If the club is presented in an enthusiastic manner, the students are more likely to want to participate.

The students who volunteer for the program should be given plenty of praise. Working with children with autism can be discouraging at times. To maintain the peers' interest in participating in the Friends Club, you must tell the peers that they are doing something that will help everybody in the class (including the target child). The students also need to understand that there will be plenty of teacher support. The teacher will immediately address any questions or concerns the students have during their turns as peer buddies.

Step Three: Implement the program

The children should be taught several things before they start playing with the target child.

Methods in redirection

When the target child is doing something inappropriate, the peer may need to be the one to suggest appropriate things to do together. The same holds true for an inappropriate conversation. Changing the topic or expressing the desire to talk about something else is a way for the buddy to turn an inappropriate interaction into an appropriate one. The peer buddy may need to gently take the target child's hand, or use a visual cue, pointing, demonstrating, etc., to get the attention of the target child. This is fine when done gently—not in a forceful manner, but in a guiding way. The peers may need guidance from the teacher as to when to redirect, what is the best method; etc., until they become comfortable with it.

How to handle a refusal

Peers should understand that the child with autism may not always want to play with them. The peer buddy needs to understand that this is not personal, and there is nothing that he or she is doing wrong. It is just that children with autism sometimes prefer to play alone. If this happens, the peer should try to redirect first. If after a few unsuccessful tries, the peer should leave and try again later.

How to gain eye contact

The peer may not realize how important eye contact is. Explain that a simple command, "Look at me," or "Show me your eyes," can be effective in increasing the attention they get from the target child. Without eye contact, the target child is less likely to know what the peer is saying or doing.

How to encourage language

The students must understand that smiling and laughing when working or playing with the target child can be very effective in gaining attention and encouraging language. The students should first get the child's attention by being close to him or her, saying the child's name, and making sure that the child is looking at what he or she is playing with. Once the child with autism is attending to the peer buddy, the peer can then ask questions, make comments, and obtain answers from his or her friend.

How to draw students into what they are playing

Social invitations, such as, "Come play with me," or "Let's go," are sometimes enough to encourage the target child to join others in the activity. Other times, it takes a gentle pull on the arm or pat on the back to get participation. When playing in certain areas, or with certain toys, it helps to show the target child how to play. The target child learns from watching typical models. Statements such as, "Look, I can slide like this," or "Watch me roll the truck," could help encourage an uninterested child. The peer buddy's enthusiasm will help the target child to become interested in the activity. Statements like "Wow, look at that truck!" or "Watch how fast I can slide," create an exciting and inviting atmosphere for playing.

Step Four: Keeping the peer buddies happy

Many times a peer buddy will become discouraged due to the lack of interest shown by the child with autism. High levels of praise and encouragement are necessary to keep the peer buddies motivated. You may need to set up a reward system to add a little incentive to the program. A sticker, special treat, or favored activity usually make good rewards. Be sure to listen to and address the specific complaints of the peer models. There may be problems with the environment that could be eliminated by a simple change. The teacher should make it as easy as possible for the peers to play with the target child.

Periodically, a discussion-group meeting should be held for the students participating in the Friends Club. At this time, the students have the chance to share the good things that happened, as well as voice any concerns about the program. This is a great time to give the students positive reinforcement for their participation in the club. As the children discuss experiences with each other, they learn what works and what does not work. The students serve as support and encouragement for each other, as well as gaining support from the teacher. The skills the peer models learn through this program are helpful in all relationships, not just the one they are developing with the target child.

At the end of the year, teachers may wish to send home a certificate stating that the child graduated from the ___grade Friends Club. This is an added motivator for children, which may well be an incentive for them to become involved in similar programs the next year. Sensitivity and caring for others who have disabilities are necessary components to children and adult lives. The Friends Club can be a positive program working toward that goal.

Peer Tutoring Programs for Children with Autism

Peer tutoring programs are successfully used across the nation to improve the programming of children with autism. Teachers find that children with autism and pervasive developmental disorders can often learn social cues and nuances easier and quicker from positive peer models than from direct teacher instruction. Along with the gains social skills training can provide, peer tutors can provide remedial instruction in academics.

A peer tutor program allows for a non-disabled, age-level student to conduct social and educational training with a child with a disability. The peer models are volunteers from classmates in elementary schools. The criteria for involvement by the peer tutor varies, but in all cases, the student must exhibit positive social skills, along with having the understanding of the current academics being taught. It is helpful if the student is fairly popular and has a wide selection of friends to offer opportunities for social gatherings for the child with the disability. Incentives for the peer tutor can be special awards or privileges.

Peer tutor programs are as varied as individual schools. High schools often have the peer tutoring programs that involve credit towards graduation for its volunteers. Elementary schools often have more informal, social-related programs to teach the child appropriate behaviors during classroom time. They encourage social interaction during recess or group time, as well as offer remedial help with academics. It is often easier to impact the academic and social skills of a kindergarten or early elementary student with autism than it is for that same student who has reached the upper elementary or secondary school grades. The younger child often will have fewer behaviors and experiences that might interfere with the training. For this reason, children who are in the early school years (who are identified with a pervasive developmental disorder) should have a peer tutor program as part of their daily curriculum.

With a child with autism, academic abilities may vary from severely delayed to grade-equivalent, but the social abilities will most likely lag. Therefore, it is imperative to start as early as possible to teach the child the social skills that are necessary. Social skills training has not typically been a part of the educational process, but the importance of appropriate social skills cannot be underestimated because of its impact on all aspects of life. Children with pervasive developmental disorders do not have a general understanding of the social domain; however, with the help of peer models and tutors, they can learn how to react to social situations using learned phrases and routines. Children who have had this training in the early school years can use these skills throughout their educational years.

Step One: Identify target child's areas of strengths and weaknesses

Look at the child's skills that may be capitalized in the program, identify problem behaviors and the incompatible behaviors, and identify possible reinforcers for use with the program. Determine academic level strengths and weaknesses.

Step Two: Identify areas in which the peer tutor will work with the child

Identify which areas need improvement: academic, social skills, classroom rules, etc. Also, identify timeframes that the peer tutor should be available to the child with autism. If social skills are to be addressed, then the peer should be paired with the target child during center time, group projects, show and tell, calendar time, etc. Any time that is less structured with ample opportunities for interactions should be considered for a peer tutor assignment. If academic skills need to be addressed, then the peer should be assigned during math time, reading time, etc.

Step Three: Identify the peer tutors

Training several peer tutors who can rotate days or training a group of children so that the target child may choose among them is convenient. However, if the target child does the choosing, then teacher supervision may be necessary to ensure everyone gets chosen over the weeks or months the program is in operation. A simple chart can alleviate this problem. Entire classes can be trained and a Friends Club can be implemented where one name is drawn out of a container each time a tutor is needed.

Friends Clubs work very well in the elementary school years. The children will likely quickly volunteer to be a part of the Friends Club if they are given information about the disability and asked to be an important part of the program. A word of caution: before the disability of autism is identified to peers, you must obtain the permission of the parents. Some parents do not want the disability to be known to classmates. If this is the case, then a Friends Club can still be set up for the entire class. The teacher can explain that everyone needs help in some areas, including reading, math, play skills, etc., and then draw out names, as needed, for all the children. Typical children can also benefit by having an occasional peer tutor.

Step Four: Training the peer tutor

During the peer tutor training, the target child should not be in attendance. This is the time to cover child-specific behaviors, redirection , cueing methods, etc. It is also helpful to give basic information on autism. Everyone needs to know why the child is having difficulty in certain areas, and why they need the extra help. However, the explanation should be kept very simple, eliminating technical or confusing terms. Allow ample opportunity for the children to ask questions. This will give the teacher a fairly accurate assessment of their knowledge and opinions of disabilities in general.

Step Five: Beginning the program

The teacher should take the target child aside (usually on a Friday) and explain that starting on Monday, he or she will now have a helper during all (or part) of the day. Explain that the peer tutor will be there to answer questions and explain what is happening, but the peer will not be doing the work for the targeted student. Show the student the chart of names to choose from (if that was the chosen method). Keep all of this talk on a positive note and use visual methods to help explain. The peer tutor should have the privilege of changing his or her seating arrangement in order to sit next to the target child during the day. The target child's seating position should stay the same to prevent problems with transitions.

Step Six: Tips to remember during implementation

The target child may have problem behaviors that do not seem to be affected by the peer tutor programming. In these instances, teachers may want to employ further behavior modification techniques to eliminate stubborn, inappropriate behaviors. These techniques can include earning stars during the day for following certain rules and then getting a treat at the end of the day, etc

There may also be times when the child does not want the peer tutor at all. In those instances, teachers may want to give him or her the option of having one day a week with no peer tutor, but the child understands that on the other days, a peer tutor will be available. Time spans of the peer tutor may have to be increased gradually in order to increase the tolerance level of the target child. Also, analyzing reinforcers, peer tutors and teaching methods may be helpful in pinpointing the lack of motivation on the part of the target child.

Peer tutors need a lot of encouragement from the teacher. Small reinforcers that can be earned by the tutors can be helpful—notes to parents about their endeavors, star charts, or stickers for the time spent in helping someone else—can go a long way to keeping the peer motivated. It is important to keep the enthusiasm high for the program to make the most impact.

You must periodically reassess the need for extra help in the chosen areas. Academics may improve enough to select other areas on which to concentrate. Social skills may improve enough to change the skill level; however, the child with autism will probably always need some form of peer modeling for social skills. This area should not be abandoned readily.

Peer tutoring programs have had a large impact on educational programs for children with autism. Programs that may have been beyond the capabilities of the child with autism are now open for learning new experiences and opportunities. The exposure to typical children acting as peer tutors can enhance any IEP objective for the target child, as well as educate the non-disabled population on disabilities. Teachers having children with autism in their classroom should seriously consider the implementation of a peer tutor program.

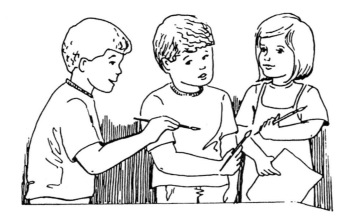

The Classroom Manager Role

An Interactive Program for Students with Autism

Many teachers use their students to help them carry out day-to-day jobs, placing students into a position of responsibility. This can raise self-esteem, as well as provide a valuable service to the teacher. Examples of classroom jobs are table helper, door holder, line leader, bathroom monitor, lunch money collector, music instrument helper, message-taker, etc.

As part of the regular education classroom, we expect that our students with autism will also enjoy the added responsibility of these classroom jobs, regardless of whether they are able to accomplish them independently. However, many of the jobs are intended to be accomplished in silence and totally independent of discussion with peers.

The jobs may meet the needs of the teacher and students, but they do not frequently place the student with autism in a situation where he or she **must** interact with peers, thereby missing a valuable social and language opportunity. This is the crucial, missing component that must be addressed by all teachers of students with autism.

The issue of increasing frequency of social interaction is directly addressed in *Effects of a Classroom Manager Role on the Social Interaction Patterns and Social Status of Withdrawn Kindergarten Students*, (Sainato, D., Maheady, L., and Shook, G. L., 1986). This article discusses an example of a strategy used to place overly shy kindergarten students in situations where they have to interact with, or direct, their peers by providing them with classroom jobs that require social interaction. We have extended this method to students with autism in general education settings.

Teachers must analyze their classroom schedule and programming to include class jobs that incorporate the interactions between the students. There are many classroom jobs that can be adapted to include this component. For example, the *Milk Man Job*. A student with autism must ask each child going into the lunchroom which type of milk does he or she want. "Do you want white milk or chocolate milk?" The student can then get the milk requested, hand it to the student, respond to the student's "thank you," and go to the next child. Possible objectives addressed during this interaction are eye gaze, vocal tone, expressive language, receptive language, listening, following through with directive, proximity, gestural use, etc.

Another classroom manager role can be the teacher's helper. During one position as teacher's helper, the student can hand out student papers to everyone in the class by reading the name on the paper, identifying the student, stating the student's name, and saying "Good job" or "Congratulations!" (or any number of reinforcing comments). During center time (or family time), a student's job could be to ask certain children to share their thoughts or feelings about a particular subject, ask personal questions (such as how many siblings that student has, whether he or she has a pet, what the pet's name is, etc.). In this way, the student is again placed in a position of having to interact with peers.

The "message taker" can deliver a message to the front office by walking down with a peer, delivering the message, asking the peer to help him or her remember the answer, etc. The walk down to the office can be rich in peer-to-peer interactions.

Using this strategy, students with autism will be able to take advantage of all the "naturally" occurring and orchestrated situations that take place among students that will directly address pragmatic language and social interaction. Too often, our students do not have this excellent opportunity, missing many golden "teachable moments." Under the guise of the classroom manager role, students with autism will have numerous, daily opportunities to affect their social and language goals and have a better chance to improve overall social and language functioning.

Reference

Sainato, D.; Maheady, L.; and Shook, G. L., (1986). The effects of a classroom manager role on the social interaction patterns and social status of withdrawn kindergarten students. *Journal of Applied Behavior Analysis*, 19,187-195.

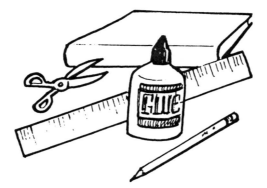

The Lunch Bunch[2]

As students with autism become more included in general education settings, it is apparent that their social skills require attention. Inappropriate social behaviors are often exhibited in classrooms, hallways, cafeterias, playgrounds, etc. These same children rarely have the opportunity to experience direct instruction of social skills under the typical curriculum, setting the stage for continued, and long-term, difficulties in these areas. Teachers everywhere have addressed direct instruction of social skills in a variety of ways, including in-class groups, pull-out modes, one-on-one instruction, small groups of disabled children, and small, integrated groups. Also, teachers have used a variety of curricula to assist them in the selection of objectives that are used in the instruction session. The EARC School-Age Program has long used the various techniques designed to address social skills, and the Inclusion Project has an overall foundation of emphasizing social skills.

The Lunch Bunch, as implemented by Debbie Griffith at Mt. Bethel Elementary School in Cobb County, Georgia, is a program based on small group instruction. It provides students with autism the opportunity to practice social skills in a small group setting under direct supervision, but without removing them from valuable, regular education classes.

The Lunch Bunch always has a facilitator. This can be any adult familiar with the students: inclusion coordinator, regular or special education teacher, paraprofessional, or school counselor/psychologist. *The Lunch Bunch* is currently used by many teachers in the EARC/Cobb County Inclusion Project, as well as by teachers in other counties. The program has proven very successful in addressing appropriate and inappropriate social behaviors.

The facilitator must familiarize the students with this concept by explaining *The Lunch Bunch* to all the students in a classroom that has been chosen ahead of time (a classroom that has a student with autism). The program should be presented as an exciting opportunity for the students to "get together" with their friends and classmates, to have lunch to discuss a chosen topic, or to have a mini-party. The facilitator must make every effort to heighten the students' enthusiasm for participation. The facilitator can tell the students that at the end of every *Lunch Bunch*, all of them will receive a small prize or treat.

Prior to implementation of *The Lunch Bunch*

Prior to implementing *The Lunch Bunch*, the facilitator should conduct a social skills assessment on each student with autism who is selected for participation in the program. Examples of assessment instruments include *Skillstreaming* (by Research Press), the *Walker*

---

[2] Thanks to Mt. Bethel Elementary School and D. Griffith of Cobb County, GA

Social Skills Curriculum (by Pro-Ed), or the *Walker-McConnell Scale of Social Competence and School Adjustment* (by Singular Publishing Group, Inc.). The results of these rating forms will guide the selection of objectives for each child and help the facilitator organize the structure of *The Lunch Bunch*.

Structure of *The Lunch Bunch*

At the beginning of each *Lunch Bunch*, the facilitator should ask the target student to choose three or four friends to participate. Teachers have used many methods to choose these children, including rotation, placing names in a jar and having a child choose the names, choosing the first three or four students who have their work finished, etc. Regardless of the method, it is important to make sure that all students get a chance to participate because many typical peers also need assistance in developing appropriate social skills.

The Lunch Bunch is best conducted in a secluded setting (away from distractions). First, the students go to the cafeteria to get their trays and then proceed to the designated classroom or other unoccupied room or area (e.g., adult conference room, media center, playground, etc.). While the students eat, the facilitator can run games or promote interactive conversations around a specific topic that targets the chosen social skill objective.

An excellent procedure for *The Lunch Bunch* is to introduce the chosen topic, allow the students to discuss the topic (with monitoring by the facilitator), and when the students have finished eating lunch, conduct a small group game. At the end of *The Lunch Bunch* and before the students return their trays, the facilitator should give out a small treat to each child (stickers, edible treats, smiley faces, McDonald's-size prizes, certificates, etc.). This will help to keep the children excited about *The Lunch Bunch* and will encourage others to want to attend.

Each target child should participate in this program once a week. In settings where the facilitator has several students with autism (for example, an inclusion coordinator in a demonstration site), then he or she should rotate the students as quickly as possible by having a *Lunch Bunch* every day (of course, this will depend on staff availability).

A selection of games and goals are included in this book. Teachers may find other games that may prove helpful in conducting *The Lunch Bunch*, as it is important to eliminate burn-out when playing the games.

Social Games for Elementary Students

Typical students develop many social skills during unstructured social time, such as recess and lunch. However, for students with autism, it is often this is the time that is most difficult for them to work on appropriate skills. The lack of structure and the difficulty with social interactions often leave students with autism isolated during the very times that can offer tremendous opportunities for social development.

Teachers and paraprofessionals (or parent volunteers) can help students with autism develop social skills by adding structure to an otherwise unstructured social time like recess or lunch (see *Lunch Bunch*). Conducting structured social games can help these students learn appropriate interaction skills, as well as build their repertoire of appropriate ways to play.

Below is a selection of games that have proven successful at promoting social interaction and teaching much-needed social skills to students with autism. Included are skills that the facilitator should target during the games. The facilitator should provide assistance when needed, but refrain from interrupting any natural social interaction that may occur during the session. Remember, many directions and cues can be better provided by a peer than an adult.

Low-Activity-Level Games

Go Fish

Children take turns playing this popular card game. Facilitator should target requesting skills, eye contact, turn-taking, and using other students' names.

Puzzles

The children work together to assemble one large puzzle. The facilitator should target the skills of working together, requesting or offering help, and watching peers.

Operator

The children sit in a circle. The facilitator whispers a message to the first child, and the child passes the message around the circle. The final message will be distorted and funny. Facilitator should target listening skills.

Hot or Cold

Children search for a hidden object by moving around and asking, "Hot or cold?" Closer to the object is hot and farther away is cold. The facilitator should target attending skills, following directions, and reasoning skills.

I Spy

The leader describes something in plain sight and the other students have to guess what the object is by asking questions to expand on the basic information. Facilitator should target attending to visual cues and listening skills.

20 Questions

Children must guess what object the leader is thinking of in 20 questions or less. If they succeed, it is their turn to think of the next object. If not, the leader gets another turn. The facilitator should target listening skills, language skills, and reasoning skills.

Going to the Market

Children take turns saying, "I'm going to the market to buy some ____." Each child has to repeat what has already been said and add a new item. The facilitator should target listening skills, memory skills, and turn-taking.

Who Am I?

One child covers his ears as the other students decide which famous person or character the child represents. He then has to guess who he is from clues given by his peers. The facilitator should target listening and reasoning skills.

High-Activity-Level Games

Blob

Children move around the space. The facilitator yells out a number, and the children need to get in a group (Blob) with that many children. The culmination of this game should be a group with all the students. Facilitator should target toleration of proximity to peers, listening skills, and cooperation.

Freeze Tag

Several children are "It" and try to tag the rest of the students. Once tagged, the students must stand frozen in place. To get unfrozen, another child must crawl between the frozen student's legs without getting tagged him or herself. The goal of this game is to keep everyone unfrozen. Facilitator should target turn taking, cooperation, and physical activity.

Charades

Children take turns acting out animals or characters. Other students work together to guess what animal or character is being portrayed. The facilitator should target watching peers and imagination skills.

Do What I Do

Students pair off and face each other, almost touching. One student starts by moving his body slowly, and the other student must copy the movement exactly. Then, the other student gets to move. The facilitator should target watching, imitation, turn-taking, and proximity to peers.

Do What I Say

The facilitator narrates a story while children act out the roles, each playing a character in the story. The students can take turns narrating the story, and with each new narrator, the story can take a new direction. The facilitator can target listening skills, imaginative play, and language skills.

Most common children's games[3] (including Hide and Seek; Red Light, Green Light; Mother May I; and Simon Says) work well as long as the facilitator has goals in mind for the target student. Common goals in these games include: listening skills, watching peers, cooperation, gross-motor skills, and turn-taking. It may be a good idea to pair students up so that they are working in teams. This gives the target student more opportunities to interact with typical peers and lowers the competitive nature of many of these popular games.

---

[3] The majority of these games are traditional, and most adults and children will be familiar with them.

Rehearsal Strategies for Teaching Appropriate Social Skills

Many students with autism demonstrate inappropriate behaviors in unfamiliar or highly stressful situations. These students are often unable to generalize previously learned skills to new situations the way typical students do, and therefore have to learn appropriate responses to each situation individually. In addition, some situations are so stressful or difficult (social interaction rarely comes "naturally" to children with autism) that repeated exposure to these situations is needed to truly teach appropriate responses. Using rehearsal strategies is one way to teach appropriate coping skills for stressful or novel situations, as well as appropriate social skills.

One type of rehearsal strategy that is a staple of special education teaching strategies is to put the anxiety-provoking, or new situation into a story format and have the student read the story prior to the event. Carol Gray has outlined this particular strategy in her *Social Stories* books, which many teachers find helpful. Social stories can be beneficial because they put social situations in ways students with autism can understand; the perspective of the story is through the eyes of the child with autism. An additional benefit of this style of teaching is that the stories can be flexible to include individual classroom situations and activities, and peers can help to implement them, thereby increasing opportunities for social interactions

Another rehearsal strategy can be role-playing appropriate social situations with or without videotaped scenes. Students can rehearse situations before the actual encounter. The teacher can talk the student through the situation explaining what will be happening and how the student should react.

Cue cards with steps that the student is to go over can be quite simple and fit in pockets; or they can be large, poster-style formats hung on a wall. Peer helpers can also help the students rehearse their steps and remind them of what they are to be doing or thinking.

The key to rehearsal strategies is that the same situation is rehearsed many times until it is no longer stressful or it becomes familiar. Even after practicing a situation, a student with autism may still need support during the actual event.

Reference

Gray, C. (1994). The Social Story Kit: writing for students with autism and related disorders. Future Horizons Inc., Arlington, Texas.

How Do We Impact Behavior?

Inappropriate Behaviors in Students with Autism

Where Do We Start?

Students with autism exhibit behaviors that baffle and frustrate our efforts to teach them. Frequently, teachers try to control or eliminate inappropriate behavior without understanding its motivation. The behavior does not stop, the teacher becomes frustrated, and the student is sent home with the hope that "tomorrow will be better." Teachers can become so caught up in this cycle of trying to eliminate the behavior (without knowing or understanding why they have difficulty doing so) that teacher burn-out frequently occurs. Too often the focus becomes stopping the behavior, with the result that the behavior does not stop, and the teachers believe that the student is incapable of being taught.

Teachers and parents need to understand that behavior is rarely exhibited "out of the blue." The function of the behavior is often quite apparent after analysis, and appropriate replacement behaviors can be found. The function of behavior usually falls into four categories:

- Escape: Getting out of a demand, activity, or situation

- Make Demand: Trying to get something desired (object, activity, or attention)

- Get Attention: Trying to secure attention from adults or peers

- Self-Stimulation: Just for the fun of it; would go on if everyone left the room

The following steps are presented as an aid to the teacher or parent when they are faced with a difficult behavior that has not been eliminated by simple techniques.

Step One: Identifying expectations and directions

Are your directions clear? Are you saying the same thing that your support staff is? Do both parents agree on how to address the child? Too often, staff (or parents) are not on the same wave length, which confuses and frustrates the child. Have you identified the appropriate strategies and methods to teach this particular student? Remember, students with autism need **clear, concise directions**, and they often do better when visual back-up systems are used in conjunction with the directions. If these are all being followed and you are still seeing inappropriate behaviors exhibited, check that the environment has been eliminated as a source of frustration, and go on to the next step.

Step Two: Identifying the behavior

The second step is to actually define the behavior in objective terms. How would an unfamiliar person describe this behavior? What does it look like? Tear the behavior apart and look at the various components of it. A behavior component **must be seen to be described!**

Step Three: Preliminary data collection

The third step is to identify how often this behavior is occurs, what setting it occurs most often in, what time of day, what activity is being conducted, what people are involved, and what was the antecedent (what set off the behavior). A description of the actual behavior and the consequence resulting from that behavior is necessary to gain a complete understanding of all of the factors surrounding this behavior. A sample form for this data collection can be as simple as the following chart:

Name:_____ **Behavior being tracked:**_____

Date & Time	People	Activity	Setting	Antecedent	Description	Consequence

Data tracking should be conducted over at least two weeks to gain a true insight. Less frequent behavior exhibition can be difficult to "catch," so longer data tracking periods may be necessary.

Step Four: Analysis of the data

Several people should analyze the behavior data to gather patterns and draw conclusions. Often, a single viewpoint is not enough to find subtle patterns in behavior. Teachers who are fully involved with the student sometimes do not identify functions of behaviors that an objective person might.

Many times, you will immediately understand the motive or function of the behavior by looking at the data and making environmental changes. But usually, the process of changing behavior does not stop after the identification of the function. Too often, however, teachers stop at this point, and the data that has been collected is the result and extent of the analysis of the behavior (and is the main reason behavior returns or reappears in a different form). You **must** go on to the next step!

Step Five: If you don't like the behavior...

If you do not like the behavior the student used to tell you what he or she wanted (whatever the function identified), **what do you want the student to do instead?** The behavior was exhibited for a **definite, legitimate reason** (for the student), so you **must** provide him or her with a different way to ask for that object or activity.. If the student had this new, more ideal behavior in his or her repertoire to obtain wants and needs, the student would have used it! Therefore, you must think of this as an area the student needs to be taught (*A Teachable Moment*). For example, if a student hits another student or tears up that student's papers, and the function was determined that the student did not like his peer to be sitting next to him, then teach your student to tell his classmate to "*Please go away.*" This is the replacement behavior that is more acceptable and eliminates the other student being hurt.

Many times, a student's behaviors are not necessarily negative in the broad sense, but they just interfere with the operation of the classroom, such as leaving the desk and wandering around the room, reading books out loud, leaving the line in the hall to look at papers taped on the wall, starting to undress in the hallway on the way to the bathroom, etc. These may not be "serious" behaviors, but they do not conform to what the rest of the class is doing (or may prove embarrassing). Students with autism often just do not understand, or "pick up on," the more subtle cues that teachers present to typical students, and therefore "march to a different drummer" Again, if you don't like the behavior the student is exhibiting, *then what do you want instead?* Identify the opposite, replacement behavior that will need to be taught to the student. For example, for the student who wanders away from the line in the hallways, your replacement behavior is to *stay behind _____ (peer) in the line.* Instead of reading books out loud, your targeted behavior becomes *reading books silently.* Instead of beginning to undress on the way to the bathroom, teach the student that he *unsnaps his pants when he gets to the bathroom.*

Targeted behaviors take on a whole new meaning. You are no longer targeting the inappropriate behavior (though you will continue to track it with data collection). Instead, target the new, appropriate behaviors. The student's targeted behavior list should **not** include a list of inappropriate behaviors, but should include the list of behaviors that are the more appropriate version!

Step Six: How do I get the student to do this wonderful, new behavior?

Demonstrating, modeling, and reinforcing! **Everyone** changes behavior when he or she needs or wants to. Students with autism often need to be taught what the desirable, replacement behavior is that everyone wants. They probably do not understand why the new behavior should be exhibited instead of the old! Therefore, we have to provide them with a rational motive for changing the behavior, regardless of whether they understand the reason or not. External motivators should be as close to the natural motivator and appropriate to the task as possible. However, sometimes that is not possible, and we look for other motivators.

Conducting motivational surveys can provide you with a number of preferred objects, activities, etc., that can be used to encourage this new behavior. There are, essentially, three levels of reinforcers: primary (food, drink, warmth, comfort, etc.), secondary (checks, stickers, points, walks in the hallway, etc.), and intrinsic (social attention, praise, pride in accomplishment, etc.). Students with autism are often unmotivated by the intrinsic level reinforcers, and teachers (and parents) must look toward the secondary or primary levels to gain the child's understanding of why the new behavior is better than the old.

You also get the student to do this "wonderful new behavior" by providing **lots** of opportunities to do so! The student will not understand what you are teaching or the reasons behind it if he or she only gets the chance to do it once per day or week. If possible, set up many opportunities to display this new behavior instead of the old, so that the student may receive the reinforcer many times during the day. Only then will the student begin to pair the two together (new behavior and the reinforcer). It will become more desirable for him or her to exhibit the more appropriate behavior than the inappropriate behavior, and you now have behavior change!

Summary:

To summarize, the steps in behavior change include the following:

- define and clarify expectations

- eliminate environment as a source of frustration

- identify the actual behavior

- collect data

- analyze the data

- identify what you want the student to do instead

- identify a motivator to encourage the replacement behavior

Eliminating a negative behavior is only half of the problem facing teachers. The other half consists of deciding what the **replacement** behavior should be and what the **reinforcer** should be for exhibiting this new, desirable behavior. Once these issues have been decided, it will be easier for all to remember what they are to reinforce. Remembering this formula will help you in problem-solving the situation. It doesn't mean that it will always be easy to effect the behavior change. If the behavior is resistant to all that you have tried, then look to the reinforcer and the number of opportunities to exhibit the new behavior. If the reinforcer chosen does not encourage the change in behavior, then **it is not a reinforcer!** And if the student never gets a chance to try the new behavior over and over again, then it will be very difficult to have him place this routine in his long-term memory banks. Re-analyze the motivators and intervals and try again! Learning the appropriate behaviors is <u>always</u> worth the effort!

Behavior Terms and Definitions

The following terms may help to clarify behavior management strategies for your classroom.

Differential Reinforcement of Other Behaviors (DRO)

This is the method of reinforcing a child for not exhibiting the inappropriate behavior for a specified period of time. Other terms used for DRO are differential reinforcement of zero rates of behavior, or differential reinforcement of the omission of behavior.

> Example: A child is reinforced for not talking out of turn in a ten-minute session during reading class.

Differential Reinforcement of Incompatible Behaviors (DRI)

This is when the child is reinforced for exhibiting a behavior that physically, or emotionally, cannot be exhibited at the same time as the inappropriate behavior.

> Example: Reinforcing a child for in-seat behavior (which cannot occur simultaneously with out-of-seat behavior).

Differential Reinforcement of Alternative Behaviors (DRA)

This method involves reinforcing a more appropriate behavior that the teachers or parents wish the child to learn, instead of exhibiting the inappropriate behavior.

> Example: Reinforcing the child's use of an alternative communication system instead of crying and screaming when making requests.

Differential Reinforcement of Lower Rates of Behavior (DRL)

This method involves reinforcing the child for exhibiting a number of responses in a specified period of time that is less than, or equal to, a prescribed limit.

> Example: Reinforcing a child for having one less tantrum than the day before.

Negative Reinforcement

This is a method that involves the removal of an aversive stimulus (something the child dislikes) immediately following the required appropriate response. The student performs the required behavior to **escape** the aversive stimulus.

> Example: The child increases appropriate behavior because he or she is trying to avoid getting a negative checkmark on the board.

Extinction

Extinction is when the reinforcer sustaining an inappropriate behavior is abruptly withdrawn. Extinction is often used in conjunction with DRA.

> Example: Ignoring a child's attempts to gain attention.

Problems with extinction: You cannot put dangerous behaviors on extinction such as self-injurious behavior (SIB) and aggression. You may get an extinction burst when using it. The effects of extinction are often not immediate, and you cannot always generalize the effects. In addition, extinction can be **extremely** difficult to do effectively in a classroom for long. Try to avoid this method unless you can control **all** of the attention-seeking components!

Motivation and Children with Autism

A Regular Education Experience

All children in school require varying levels of motivation during their school day to accomplish the tasks presented to them. Teachers use a variety of methods when applying motivators to their lessons. For example, teachers award grades (A, B, C, etc.), use check marks when an assignment is done, draw happy faces on papers that have met with teacher approval, apply stickers, etc. Children, for the most part, readily accept these reinforcers for good work and strive to do their best in order to obtain them. However, for some children, such as children with autism, many of the motivators that teachers use do not accomplish the task of motivation. Children with autism are often not reinforced by the standard selection of reinforcers that the teachers have at hand. The teacher of a child with autism must look beyond the norm and gather objects and activities that will encourage his or her participation in various tasks and assignments.

Motivation is very individually specific. We are all motivated by different things. One person may find a specific restaurant very good and drive long distances just to get to it. To this person, it can be highly motivating, while to someone else, it may not mean anything.

Children with autism are similar in having the ability to be motivated, but the objects for which they are motivated may not be something that another child finds attractive. A piece of string could fascinate a child with autism for hours when there is no logical reason for it to do so. On the other hand, a game that typical children generally love to play may hold no interest to a child with autism.

Motivation can be a powerful tool in teaching a child. When the child is interested in something, it is easier to teach using the child's interest. For example, if the student loves sand, the target child can be paired with a peer at the sand table. That target child will be more likely to interact with the peer at the sand table than at the art table, because the target child doesn't care about art. A good way to encourage social skills is to give favored toys for the target child to play with, but only if he or she will share with another child.

If the child is motivated by sand, but the class schedule denotes that it is time for art, the sand table can be used as a reinforcer. The teacher can say, "After you finish your art project, you may play at the sand table." This will help motivate the child to complete the art project in order to earn the sand table. The sand table becomes a powerful reinforcer.

Through the use of behavior charts, the teacher can use a reinforcing motivator to gain cooperation and good behavior throughout the day. The student can earn stars for certain activities or time periods for following teacher direction, sharing materials, sitting quietly in his or her seat, etc.

You can place "stars" on any number of behavior charts; for example, place petals on a flower or give carrots to a rabbit. You can also fill in squares on a page. The child earns the motivator for accomplishing the task. Once the chart is full, the student may earn an additional reward, such as hanging the picture on the wall, getting to put the chart in a special book, carrying it home to show parents, etc. The entire *Rocket Ship* program is based on the student wanting to earn his or her way to the top to *Blast Off*! This appears to be a highly reinforcing motivator to the child, as well as a method to teach new behavior.

Motivators often change with a child with autism. What was motivating one week may not be motivating the next. It is important that we make sure the reinforcements being used in the classroom setting are indeed motivating to the student. If a particular motivator has lost its power with the child, it will no longer be reinforcing enough for the child to comply with the teacher's direction. To keep the motivators interesting for longer periods, it usually helps to limit one reinforcer to one activity and to change the selection often. For example:

- When Joey finishes his art project, he can play at the sand table

- When Joey finishes spelling, he can listen to headphones

- When Joey finishes reading, he can use his special marker, etc.

With some children with autism, verbal cues may not be enough. Verbally telling the child that he or she can play with the sand table after earning three stars may not enable the child to fully understand. A visual cue, such as posting a star chart (depicting the sand table) on his or her desk may help. In this way, the child can see the actual reinforcer and understand what he or she is working toward.

When teaching new skills to a child with autism, a reinforcer motivating the child may also be used to encourage participation in group activities. This gives the teacher a positive, rather than negative, method for gaining the child's cooperation, which is then used in teaching valuable social or behavioral skills.

Many times, instead of earning a reinforcer, children lose privileges or receive discipline for inappropriate behaviors. Often, they do not understand what it is they have done wrong. The more negatively based method does not teach the positive behavior that the teacher expects.

For example: Stevie loses points for talking out-of-turn. With this method, he is not being taught to raise his hand when he wants to speak. If children do not understand what they have done wrong, they cannot attempt to change their behavior. This does not teach them anything. If they get rewarded for doing something right, they know what to repeat in order to get the same reinforcing motivator again. The key for encouraging good behavior is to find what is reinforcing enough to the children so that they will want to repeat that positive behavior over and over again.

Often, children with autism are motivated by very unusual objects or activities. These are not necessarily inappropriate for the classroom, but the teacher must judge them individually. The teacher may wish to use the object as a method to gain cooperation and bring the time allotted to that object under the teacher's control. Then, the time limits for playing with that object can be lessened while the teacher finds more appropriate motivators for the child. In this manner, the child's inappropriate motivator is faded out over time and is replaced by more appropriate objects. The time span allotted for this fading-out process must be judged by the teacher because to fade too quickly can create great stress and anxiety. To fade too slowly, the child will not gain new motivators in a timely fashion to be used in teaching.

Children with autism can be motivated to learn like every other child in our schools. However, they may need more attention paid to their motivators in order to gain the cooperation needed for learning. Teachers must be creative and flexible, and be willing to analyze the individual child. Children with autism are well worth the time and effort that teachers may need to spend when they are in our classrooms.

Blast Off with the *Rocket Ship*

The *Rocket Ship* forms, which can be found in the Appendix, are just one of the methods used by the EARC Inclusion Project to help students build the appropriate behaviors needed for the regular education classroom and help them to become motivated to learn. Many regular education teachers do not have time to implement long or involved behavior plans. They require simple methods that are clear, precise, and positive in nature to quickly make behavioral changes. The *Rocket Ship* plan has proven to be very effective.

Several steps are in this positive system. One *Rocket Ship* form has had the components numbered for easier explanation. Blank *Rocket Ship* forms are for you to copy for your use. Explanations will seem confusing until you have read the entire explanation. However, once you understand the components, the *Rocket Ship* is easy to implement.

Rocket Ship #1:

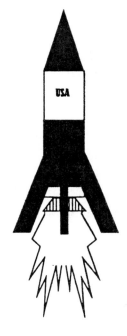

Under the **Rules**, there are three spaces for you to write what **positive** behaviors you want the student to exhibit. For example:

1. Keep hands and feet to yourself

2. Finish class work

3. Use inside voice, etc.

Do not add more than three rules because this becomes too oppressive for the student. Always state the rules in a positive manner—never in a negative manner. After you are sure that the student understands each of these rules, write them next to the large 1, 2, and 3 on the left side of the page.

Choice of the Day (top right corner of the page)

This is where you identify the large reinforcer that the student earns at the end of the *Rocket Ship* (what the student earns when he or she *Blasts Off!*). After the child has earned all of the levels, regardless of how long that takes, then the reinforcer is delivered to the child. This reinforcer must be **very** strong to encourage the student to exhibit the appropriate skills you have outlined. The student **cannot** have access to the reinforcer except when he or she has completed the *Rocket Ship*. (You may wish to conduct a Motivational Survey to aid in the identification of preferred activities and objects.)

Note: The "choice of the day" (whatever you choose as the reinforcement) must be solely reserved for the program. **The student must not have access to it at any other time**. This maintains the strength of the preferred activity for use in the *Rocket Ship*.

The lines on the right side of the page next to each level of the *Rocket Ship* are for you to write in the activities that are conducted during that time frame (see below). This should be written in pencil because you will have to erase this and write in another activity if the child does not earn that particular level.

Main body of the *Rocket Ship*

Each segment of the *Rocket Ship* denotes an interval of time. For example, the bottom interval can be reading, the next one math, the next one P.E., then Center time, lunch, art, music, nap, recess, etc. The teacher sets these intervals, and the intervals are usually as long as the activity. However, the teacher can adjust the intervals. Each segment can also be divided to increase the number of intervals in the day, or the line erased with white-out to eliminate intervals, if needed. You want the intervals to be in a reasonable timeframe for the student, but try to have the total number of intervals stretch to have the student reach the *Blast Off!* at the middle or end of the day. This will make it easier for you. The student's ability levels, coping strategies, response to the system, etc, will determine this.

Smash Up!

When a student does not earn a particular interval (make sure you are a little lenient in the beginning and give at least two warnings to get the student to understand the system), then place that interval into the *Smash Up* box. It is erased from the line above next to its appropriate interval and transferred into the *Smash Up* box to let the student (and parent) know that he or she was not able to follow the rules during that timeframe. Once you erase the interval from the line above, make sure that you write in another activity on the same line. (You may go on to the next activity in line or an alternative that you ask the student to do until the peers are finished with their work).

Make sure you do **not** leave an interval blank. When the student reaches the top of the *Rocket Ship*, <u>all intervals must have been used.</u> Placing failed intervals into the *Smash Up* box will help the student to understand that he or she was not following the rules at that particular time, but shows there is another chance with the next activity.

Bonus Box

The *Bonus Box* can be drawn in by hand, if needed. For example, you may have a time when it is clear that the student is **not** going to get to the top, and it is at the end of the day, so you cannot add any more intervals. You then hand-draw the *Bonus Box* in, tell the student that if he or she can follow the rules while collecting his or her backpack, walking to the bus, waiting for the bus, etc., then you will give the student a bonus point in the *Bonus Box*. Tell the student that he or she can fill in the first level (at the bottom of the new *Rocket Ship*) upon arriving at class the next day.

In this way, you encourage the child to be positive about one aspect of the *Rocket Ship*, you allow the student a last opportunity to show you that he or she can work hard to follow the rules, and you provide the incentive to prove that the student can demonstrate appropriate behaviors. (Plus, you will likely have a better-behaved student leaving the building than one who is very upset about not earning the *Rocket Ship*!).

The *Rocket Ship* form is sent home each evening for the parents to sign and send back to school. This gives them information about their child's behavior during the day, provides them opportunities to ask the child about his or her behaviors, activities, etc., that occurred, and also builds self-esteem in the student by the parents being proud of his or her work.

Notes:

When starting the *Rocket Ship* program, make sure that the student is able to *Blast-Off* every day for a minimum of one week. Many students will not understand the system unless they have positive experiences associated with it, and the motivation is very high. During the time that you want them to "buy into" the program, provide many reminders, praise, warnings (as necessary), etc., to make sure that they will be able to complete the *Rocket Ship* and earn the reinforcer. Also, in the beginning, the reinforcers must be the strongest possible. Enlist the aid of the parents to help you identify possible objects or activities.

Once the child has "earned" the reinforcer, he or she must not have unlimited access to it (e.g., thirty minutes of computer time). Allow an appropriate time to enjoy it, but not so much that the reinforcer starts losing its power. You may have to set a timer to denote exactly how much time has been earned with the reward. Winning computer time at school should be no more than ten minutes (fifteen at the most). At home, fifteen or twenty minutes is appropriate. After that, have the student turn the computer off and remove the games.

Have a "selection" of reinforcers that the student may choose from at the start of the day. Put them away (but within view) up on a high shelf, if possible, to remind the student about what he or she is earning.

When the first activity of the day (first interval) is over, go over the rules with the student and say, "Your first rocket stage is over. Did you follow all of your rules?" When the student says, "Yes!" then say, "You can now color in that rocket stage. Do you think you can do it for the next stage, too?" Then praise the student and go on to the next interval.

At the end of each day, present the completed *Rocket Ship* to the student and tell him or her to take it home, have the parents sign it, and bring it back the next day. (You may have to prepare the parents so they can reinforce your program by talking about it, providing praise, etc.).

After the system has been firmly established, it may be time for the student to understand that he or he does not always reach the top. Teachers need to have the student understand the consequences of his or her behavior. When the student cannot possibly earn the *Blast Off!* and the reinforcer at the end of the day, provide the *Bonus Box* to help him or her get out the door to the bus, remain calm, and look forward to another chance the next day.

Always provide students with the knowledge that they can try again and give them the hope that they can earn the reinforcer the next time. **This is extremely important!!** No student's self-esteem should be diminished by this system. The student may have to face that he or she had a hard day and did not follow the rules. *However, always talk to the student about the failure and provide him or her with reassurance that you know he or she can do better the next day and Blast Off to get the reward.*

In this way, we build better, more confident students who will strive to prove that we, as teachers, are right in our belief in them. You will find that the students will work **very** hard to exhibit the appropriate behaviors!

What if all else fails and the student's behaviors do not change? If that happens, you must analyze the system. Ask the following questions of yourself and your staff:

- Are we sure the student understands the system? Does the student have the cognitive abilities to understand?

- Are we setting the student up to fail by making the intervals too long, making the *Blast Off* too far away?

- Is the reinforcer not strong enough? (By definition, then, it is **not** a reinforcer!) Reassess the reinforcements.

- Would the student's program be stronger if we added a DRL Program (Differential Reinforcement of Lower Rates of Behavior) to this system? (Awarding the students at the end of the day for having fewer *Smash Ups!* than they did the day before).

- Should we take data collection on behaviors and conduct a functional analysis of behaviors? What is the **function** of the behaviors, and how can it be incorporated into the system?

- What is the student's communication system like? Is it sufficient for the student's needs? Talk to the speech therapist.

Rocket Ship #2

In many ways, the *Rocket Ship #2* is very much like the *Rocket Ship #1*, except that each rocket stage has been divided into segments to denote the activity (or time), and then allow space to award the student a sticker, smiley face, checkmark, etc., <u>for each individual rule that is followed</u>. This differs from *Rocket Ship # 1*, which awards the child with the rocket stage for following all three rules together. *Rocket Ship #2* allows the child to realize what rules have been followed and what rules have not been followed. This gives the teacher the chance to track individual rules to see the frequency of success and failure for each rule.

At the bottom of the chart, you will still see the *Smash Up!* box, and the criteria at the bottom for when a stage is declared a *Smash Up!* Teachers may decide that a student must earn two out of the three rules to prevent an entire stage from "smashing up." Conversely, if a student is having an exceptionally difficult day, then perhaps only one rule earned is enough to go on to the next activity's stage.

The teacher should decide on the total number of boxes earned (for following the individual rules) in order for students to *Blast Off!* and get their large reinforcer for the day. Under the total number is the actual total that the student earned. This will allow the teacher to show the student exactly how he or she did that day.

Rocket Ship #3

As the student becomes better able to follow the rules of the *Rocket Ship* and is consistently *Blasting Off* each day, it may be time to begin to fade the program. As the *Rocket Ship* is faded, the student should begin to internalize the rules and need less reinforcement throughout the day. For this purpose, a weekly *Rocket Ship* has been developed. It is important not to remove the daily reinforcement too quickly, as this may result in a resurgence of inappropriate behavior. It is best to tell the student that he or she is doing so well that he or she only needs one *Rocket Ship* per week. Nevertheless, tell the students that they will continue to earn rewards for good behavior. At any point, it may be necessary to return to the daily program.

The *Rocket Ship* is designed to be very flexible and adaptable for the classroom needs, and yet is a strong positive influence on the student. The EARC Inclusion Project has found this to be very effective with students with autism and Asperger's Syndrome, because it allows for structure to the day, has the rules clearly defined, provides a strong reinforcer, and assists in building self-esteem. In fact, many typical students have also been placed on this system!

The Appendix also shows *Flower Charts* as an alternative to all of the *Rocket Ship*s. Many young, female students prefer the *Flower Chart* over the *Rocket Ship*. The *Flower Chart* is designed on the same format, so please follow the rules for the corresponding *Rocket Ship*.

The Snake Race

Many students with autism are now in inclusive settings in general education classes. One area of difficulty for many of these students, however, is maintaining attention to the task at hand. Also, because many of these students' goals involve independent learning, teaching strategies and methods must be found that can encourage their independence, without requiring teacher time nor the presence of a paraprofessional staff member.

The attached *Snake Race*, used in other programs as part of the EARC Inclusion Program, is based on known techniques. It has proven very useful for teaching independent work skills to some students with autism. This plan places the student and the teacher in competition with one another. The goal of the program is for the student to finish the race before the teacher by filling in the snake's segments, one-by-one, for each portion of completed work. The program can be instituted on either a positive reinforcement system or a negative reinforcement system.

Results for finishing first on the snake are as follows:

Positive reinforcement: Whoever finishes the race first gets a prize.

Negative reinforcement: If the teacher finishes first, the student has to complete an extra page of academic work. If the student finishes first, he does not have to do the extra work.

A positive system is usually more encouraging to the system, as when the student wins, he earns the reward that has been selected at the beginning of the work period. If the teacher wins, the student does not earn the reward (or the teacher wins the award). The negative reinforcement system can also work, but can place the student in an anxiety-provoking situation, which should be avoided.

The *Snake Race* can be used throughout the day or for each activity. It is important to assess the student's level and set an appropriate goal for the behavior plan. If the student has great difficulty staying on-task, the plan should be used for only one activity (or part of an activity) at a time. As the student's independent work skills increase, the periods of time and demands of the plan can be gradually increased, as well.

While the plan is aimed at increasing independent work skills, a variety of behaviors can be targeted. It is important to outline the expected behaviors each time the plan is used. Before beginning, the student or teacher should select an acceptable goal (reward), and it should be written on the individual behavior sheet.

The teacher should display the *Snake Race* where the student can easily see it, which is usually on the student's desk. When the student is working (or acting) appropriately, the teacher colors in a section on the student's line of the snake. The sections should be progressive, with each segment filling next to the previous one, as in a "race." When the student is not working or following directions, the teacher then colors in a section of the teacher's line. (Although some students may prefer to color in their own segments on the snake, if the teacher does the coloring of the segments, the student is less distracted from the task at hand.

The teacher responsible for coloring in the snake's segments does not necessarily need to sit next to the student for the duration of the task. The teacher should be able to move around the room as much as possible to help other students. However, the teacher must make sure to monitor the student in order to keep the "race" going.

This plan is meant to teach independent work skills. It may eventually be used as a nonverbal prompt in lieu of more intrusive teacher prompts. During the initial implementation, however, the teacher may need to use verbal prompts to redirect the student to the program and maintain his or her enthusiasm. As the student becomes used to the program, the teacher should decrease verbal prompts and rely on the nonverbal prompt of the behavior plan. Verbal praise, as long as it is not distracting, is always good.

As the student becomes more comfortable with the *Snake Race,* the teacher may ask a peer to do the race with the student instead. This will help the student learn to keep up with her/his peers and also allows the teacher more time for instruction.

Programs such as the *Snake Race* can help students with autism become more independent in their work skills and become more accepted into the general education classrooms. This program is not solely designed for the student with autism. Teachers have used it successfully with many students, both disabled and non-disabled. I hope that many teachers will find the *Snake Race* program useful for the classroom and students.

The Puzzle Piece

Too often, students with autism require external sources of motivation to attend to the task, although they do not want to "stand out" from the other students in the class. The goal of the *Puzzle Piece* program is for the student to receive an ongoing incentive to finish the task at hand and earn a reinforcer that is manageable in the regular education classroom.

The *Puzzle Piece* plan can be used throughout the day or for each activity, although it is more feasible when used per activity. Before beginning, you must first assess the student's level of independent functioning and set an appropriate goal for task completion. If the student has great difficulty staying on-task, the plan should be used for only one activity (or part of an activity) at a time. As the student's independent work skills increase, the periods of time and demands of the plan can gradually be increased to reflect growth in skills.

While the plan seeks to increase independent work skills, it can target a variety of behaviors. It is important to outline the expected behaviors each time the plan is used. Before beginning, the student should select an acceptable reward, which will be written on the behavior sheet.

The teacher should display the *Puzzle* where the student can easily see it; e.g., the student's desk. When the student is working (or acting) appropriately, the teacher approaches the student and colors one of the *Puzzle* pieces. The teacher should aim for a set time interval for each piece (e.g., for every two minutes on task, one piece is colored). The intervals should be spaced to allow the student to complete the puzzle by remaining on task for the majority of the work period. Although some students may prefer to color their own *Puzzle* pieces, they will tend to be less distracted when the teacher provides this service.

The teacher responsible for coloring in the *Puzzle* does not need to sit next to the student for the duration of the task. The teacher should move around the room as much as possible, helping other students. However, the teacher must make sure to consistently check with the student and keep the program running.

This plan is meant to teach independent work skills; therefore, the ultimate goal is to eventually use the plan as a nonverbal prompt. It is important for the teacher to limit the number of verbal prompts to keep the student on-task. During the implementation of the program, the teacher may need to use verbal prompts to redirect the student. However, as the student becomes used to the program, the teacher should decrease verbal prompts and rely on the nonverbal prompt of the behavior plan. Verbal praise, as long as it is not distracting, is always good!

Self-regulated, Calm-down Time

Many students with autism easily become over-stimulated in regular education classrooms, which can often lead to disruptive behaviors. Some students are sensitive to high activity and noise levels, as well as the increased demands experienced by the typical educational curriculum. Often students with disabilities do not have the capability to identify when they are becoming upset, leading to quick escalation of emotion and loss of self-control. In addition, they frequently have few, if any, coping strategies to help them regain control once they have become upset.

It is especially important for students with autism to learn how to prevent loss of control in inclusive classrooms. Self-regulated calm-down time teaches students to identify when they are getting upset and to use an appropriate strategy for calming down before they lose control.

A self-regulated, calm-down time is easy to implement in the regular education setting. First, the teacher should explain that everyone gets upset from time-to-time and getting upset is "OK." However, it is important for everyone to learn how to deal with these emotions.

The teacher and the student can outline some of the actions that are not appropriate to exhibit (e.g., throwing tantrums, calling names, and hitting others), as well as acceptable substitutes (e.g., taking a walk, sitting in the hall, and reading a book). The teacher should help the student decide what appropriate coping strategies will be most successful for him or her. Written (or drawn) examples of acceptable strategies should be displayed where the student can see them. This will help the student prompt himself or herself during upsetting moments.

The teacher should then identify a visible, nonverbal signal between herself/himself and the student. Some signals that have proven effective in the past include a red flag, red light, stop sign, and ticket. When the student has the signal on his or her desk, the student then has immediate permission to discontinue whatever activity is going on and engage in one of the appropriate coping strategies.

After being able to identify the precursors to losing control, the student can be in charge of placing the signal on his or her own desk. However, at the inception of this program, the student often is unable to identify when he or she is becoming upset. In this case, the teacher should closely monitor the student during times when he or she usually has difficulty (collecting data is helpful in determining difficult time periods). Then, when the teacher observes the student getting upset, the teacher places the signal on the student's desk to prompt choosing an appropriate coping strategy. This should be done before the student has lost control. The eventual goal is for the student to identify when he or she is getting upset and manipulate the signal on his or her own.

It is important to keep the signal as subtle as possible to avoid drawing attention to the student; extra attention often makes regaining control much more difficult and can be embarrassing to higher-functioning students. Additionally, this time-out should never be used as a negative consequence for losing control. It should be seen as a positive, pro-active plan. The student needs to understand that this is not punishment, but rather praise for choosing the correct behavior under difficult circumstances.

To keep the self-regulated, calm-down plan positive, the student should be reinforced for following it. The reinforcement can be built into the student's current behavior plan or can be separate. However, it is important to consistently reinforce and praise the student when he or she effectively avoids losing control when upset.

Although the teacher should encourage the use of this plan, the student should not be using it to escape demands. A strict time limit should be determined ahead of time for the coping strategy (no more than ten minutes). A timer often proves to be an effective prompt. Whatever activity the student misses when using the "cool-off time" needs to be continued when the student returns. A very strong reinforcement system usually makes it easier to get the student back on task once he or she has calmed down.

As the student becomes more effective at controlling emotions, the teacher may wish to lower the number of times the student uses the signal per day. This is especially true if the student tries to use the plan to escape demands. The teacher needs to track the number of times per day that the student uses the plan. This information should be displayed in a visual format (graphs work well) so that the student understands it.

Each day, the teacher reminds the student how many times he or she used the plan the day before and that if the student uses it less on this day, he or she will get a reward. This helps the student discriminate between different degrees of emotion and control minor upsets without the plan. The program can eventually be faded altogether as the student consistently identifies and prevents loss of control in the classroom. However, the student should be monitored for evidence of relapse, and the plan reinstated, as necessary.

Addressing Self-stimulatory Behaviors in an Inclusive Setting

Improving Acceptance Ratios for Students with Autism

Students with autism often exhibit inappropriate, self-stimulatory movements, which can draw attention from their typically developing and socially sophisticated peers. In addition, many students with Asperger's Syndrome or autism recognize that they display these self-stim behaviors and actually seek assistance in stopping the behavior. Although typical peers are often very forgiving in elementary school classrooms, middle school students and high school students are less forgiving. These students present much stricter measures to compare social behaviors, leaving the students who have milder characteristics of autism frustrated and depressed when they realize that they lack the skills designed to admit them into social groups. As a result of the recognition of the depression and social isolation, as well as how these behaviors can affect typical initiations, self-stimulatory behaviors require addressing as early as possible. By shaping these behaviors early, the student may fit better into his peer group and have increased chances of higher acceptance from the typical peers.

The following procedures have been used to reduce self-stim behaviors and increase more appropriate replacement behaviors in the general education settings. The basis of this procedure is to increase an individual's tolerance to intervals where the behavior is not exhibited, and the substitute behavior replaces the self-stim. Behaviors such as toe-walking, rocking, fidgeting in a seat, pencil flipping, etc., may not be totally disruptive to the class, but they can (and do!) set the student apart from his typical classmates. As more students with autism enjoy regular education placement, issues of self-stim behaviors take on increased importance for both the school staff and the parents. I hope this program will aid teachers in addressing self-stim behaviors with their students.

The steps here are offered as suggestions for teachers to consider when facing unusual behaviors that they wish to change or eliminate. It is wise to modify or adapt these steps for the particular student's needs. The teacher must help the student identify other behaviors that he or she can do while "waiting" out the interval. Make sure the student receives extra cues for staying on task, completing assignments, etc. This program can work in conjunction with the EARC *Rocket Ship* program or other positive, daily, behavior programs.

Step One

Explain the inappropriate behavior to the student and tell him or her what should be done instead. For example: "People don't usually walk on their tip-toes because it is bad for their legs, and it looks funny. You should walk with your heels on the ground."

Step Two

Explain to the student that it is sometimes difficult for people to control certain behaviors because they are not always aware that they are doing them. This plan will help the student become more aware of the behavior so that he or she can gain more conscious control over it.

Step Three

Tell the student that for three minutes each morning, he or she will receive a secret signal from the teacher that will remind him or her not to do this behavior. The secret signal, depending on the age and developmental level of the student, should be something small, but tangible. A younger student might prefer a small, stuffed animal. An older student might prefer a reminder written on a small piece of paper. If the student refrains from the behavior during the three minutes, he or she gets a checkmark on a behavior sheet (like those shown in this book) and earns a reward that the student has chosen ahead of time. The teacher may require the student to earn a certain number of successful, three-minute sessions before receiving the reward. The more pervasive the behavior, the more frequently the student should be rewarded.

Step Four

After the student has consistently earned a checkmark each morning for a week, the teacher should then add a second period of three minutes in the afternoon. When the student has achieved a full week of successful sessions, then the three-minute timeframe should be increased to five minutes.

Step Five

Gradually, the teacher should increase the time and number of sessions that the student must refrain from the behavior until the periods meet in the middle of the day.

Step Six

After the student consistently refrains from the behavior throughout the day, the plan can be slowly faded. However, the behavior should be monitored for evidence of a relapse. Reinstitute the plan, if necessary.

Note: Data collection is necessary to monitor the progress of the program and to encourage the student. However, it need not be intrusive or time-consuming. The following forms are suggested as examples for teachers to use and adapt to their student's particular needs.

Self-Stim Plan 1

Student Name: _____   Behavior: _____

Date: _____   Teacher: _____

Time / Sessions	Monday	Tuesday	Wednesday	Thursday	Friday	Total

Criteria #: _____

Reward: _____

Self-Stim Plan 2

Student Name: _____   Behavior: _____

Date: _____   Teacher: _____

Date_____ Time:	Monday	Tuesday	Wednesday	Thursday	Friday	Total
Session I_____						
Session II_____						
Session III_____						
Session IV_____						
Session V_____						

Time Frame: 3 min.   5 min.   Criteria #:
                          _____
                          7 min.   10 min.   Reward
                          _____
                          12 min.   15 min
                          20 min.   30 min. (increase as needed)

Desensitization Programs for Students with Autism

Many students with autism develop intense fears or nervousness over harmless events or objects. These fears can be very debilitating and may prevent the individual from functioning appropriately in the environment. Desensitization programs are designed to decrease an individual's fears or anxiety of a person, object, situation, event, or location.

A desensitization program is set up in a step-by-step process to gradually teach the individual how to cope with the fears or anxieties he or she may encounter. You can implement a desensitization plan on a variable schedule (once or twice a day, every other day, or over several months) depending on the individual's needs. Individualization of the plan may call for an increase or decrease in frequency.

Any adult familiar with the individual with autism can conduct a desensitization program. The plan can be implemented at home, school, in the community, or in any combination of the three.

Step One: Analyze and categorize the exact fear

What exactly is the individual frightened of? Is there more than one component to this fear? If there are many, it is best to address each individual component rather than expect the individual to become desensitized to several fears at once.

Step Two: Select a strong reinforcer for the individual with autism

The more choices the individual has in the selection of the reinforcer used, the more reinforcing the reward will be. **The individual should not have access to the reward unless he or she is working on the program**. This means that the adult has full control of accessing the reinforcer. Select a reasonable timeframe for the program. The time needed to desensitize a student to an anxiety-provoking event, situation, or activity depends on:

- the intensity of the fear
- the reactions to intervention
- the consistency in the implementation of the program

Outline each step of the individualized plan. Taking data will allow the adult to track progress and adjust the demands of the program accordingly. Some students with autism may benefit from viewing their own progress and may wish to track data with the adult.

Step Three: Begin to talk about the fear-provoking object or event (X) with the student

Try to find a book or movie about X and read or watch it together. Explain how X is not harmful, and why it is important to tolerate X. Talk about appropriate reactions to X. Explain to the student that each day he or she will work on becoming tolerant of X, and each day he or she will earn a reinforcer for trying. Make sure the reinforcer is delivered after every session.

Step Four: Begin to initiate brief contact with X

Give the student prior notice that he or she will be seeing X. Remind the student of acceptable behavior and the reward. If X is a place, drive by with the student and look at it. If X is a person or an object, have the individual look at it from across the room for thirty seconds. If X is a situation or activity, have the student participate in a simulated version of it in a safe, familiar environment. During this time, the individual should receive *much praise* for remaining calm and should *immediately* receive access to the reinforcer. Mark the successes on the desensitization plan so that the student can track the progress.

Step Five: Gradually increase exposure length, number of times, and intensity

The student should continue to receive praise and rewards for this behavior. As the student becomes more comfortable with X, he or she should begin to be introduced to X in the natural setting.

Step Six: When the student is able to tolerate X at an appropriate level, the plan should be faded with more and more time required to earn a reward, until the reward is no longer needed.

Reminder: Do not put the student in a position of becoming too anxious. If the student is unable to tolerate X, then the demands should be immediately lowered to a level that he or she can tolerate. This may require some back stepping, but it is necessary to do so to prevent refusal behaviors from escalating and to prevent the inappropriate behaviors associated with the event or activity from increasing.

This desensitization plan is only a format; each teacher or parent will need to modify any or all steps, according to the particular individual's needs.

Where Do We Begin?

The IEP Process

Is This Meeting Going to Last Forever?

Even though many students with autism are being educated in inclusive settings, many regular education teachers are unfamiliar with the IEP process. Because this may be the first time that they have had a special education student, we cannot realistically expect them to know everything about an IEP that a special education teacher would. Most importantly, every teacher working with a special needs child needs to understand that the IEP (Individualized Education Plan) is the legal contract between the parents and the school that outlines the student's entire educational program.

All teachers working with the student must understand and follow the goals and objectives listed in the IEP. The special education teacher who is (usually) ultimately responsible for the student's education is designated the "IEP Holder." It is this person's responsibility to make sure that the goals in the IEP are being met and the student's progress on these goals is being documented.

Teachers working with the student with autism should have regular meetings to discuss the implementation of the IEP and the student's progress. When this is not possible, the IEP Holder must meet with the teachers individually to make sure they understand the IEP, how to meet the student's goals and objectives, and to periodically assess the student's progress. The regular education teacher should also have a copy of the student's IEP readily available so that he or she can use it to guide the development of the student's academic, social, and behavioral programs.

Regular and special education teachers play a vital role in the development of the student's IEP and, thus, the student's educational program. Many teachers and parents do not have prior knowledge of all the issues related to inclusive programming that must be decided at the IEP Team Meeting. It is best if the following issues are considered, either before or during the meeting, in order to promote a successful placement. Also listed are a few general components of the IEP process for those of you unfamiliar with this process.

Format of the meeting ("What in the world is this all about?")

An IEP meeting takes place at least once a year, but the school or parent can request it any time. This meeting is considered to be legally binding, and decisions made during this meeting can be called into court and defended by school personnel. Special education meetings can last anywhere from thirty minutes to eight hours or more, and can be spread out over the course of many months. Participants at the meeting include the parents, a school administrator, and any teacher who is working with the student. A psychologist may also be present if test results have to be interpreted. In addition, the parent may bring other family members, an advocate, or a lawyer. The IEP meeting format is designated by law under the Individuals with Disabilities Education Act (IDEA), and it is to every teacher's benefit to obtain formal information on this process and become familiar with it before the IEP meeting.

Exposure to typical peers ("How much time should the students have in regular education classes?")

Ideally, for students with autism, this should be **daily** exposure. However, this depends on the individual student and must reflect the student's ability level. Some students can benefit from a full day in regular education classes; other children cannot tolerate more than a few minutes without becoming totally overwhelmed.

The IEP Team must determine the amount of exposure. We would never ask a student to be proficient in open-heart surgery unless he or she has graduated from medical school and has had exposure to direct instruction and patient-care under supervision! The same is true for learning functional social and language skills. Direct instruction and exposure to typical peers for practice is essential to learning, but supervision and monitoring amounts of exposure is essential to building success. The length of time in the regular classroom and necessary support should be discussed at the IEP meeting. (If you are unsure whether students with autism need access to typical peers, go to the beginning of this book and read the section on *Rationale*).

Teacher planning time ("How are we going to be able to collaborate?")

Teachers need some time **every day** to discuss the student's academic work with the IEP Holder. This includes the behavior plan, social and language goals, and teaching methods. Without some collaboration time, teachers feel left out in the cold. They view themselves as not having any support or direction at all in educating the student. Teachers, be sure you understand when (or if) you get some time to meet with your fellow teachers.

Paraprofessionals also need daily guidance in teaching a student with autism. Do not expect them to automatically know what to do with the child's lessons or behavior plans. Paraprofessionals are asked to do the most, receive little or no training, and are paid far below what a teacher is paid. Nevertheless, we have extremely high expectations for them and what they should accomplish with our students. They need **frequent** (if not daily) guidance from the certified teacher in order to do the best job possible.

Levels of support ("Do we really need one-on-one?")

Just because the student has autism does not always mean that the child requires one-on-one assistance from a paraprofessional for the entire day. During the meetings, you must define the specific areas in which the student will need help. Also, plan for independent functioning.

Counting of students ("How can I take another child into my class?")

After conducting inclusion projects for many years, I know that inclusion is a much easier job when the regular education classroom has low student numbers. Although this is not typically something a parent or a teacher has control over in an IEP, discuss this topic so that everyone understands the impact high numbers have on an inclusion student. Eighteen students in a kindergarten class make for an easier time than twenty-nine students!

If at all possible, the school principal should count the special need's child in the numbers of the typical students to eliminate overloading of classes. Although this is an ideal situation, it is not always possible to keep the numbers low. When the classroom numbers increase, it is better if no more than two students with autism are placed in one classroom. This prevents overloading the stress levels on teachers. Also, careful matches should be done with those two children to ensure that they will not imitate each other's behaviors.

Transition plan ("How can this student become a part of his or her new class?")

Students not fully included should have a transition plan in place that will allow for increasing amounts of time in regular education. This builds toward full inclusion. The amount of time should be determined by multiple criteria; some behavioral, some social, and some academic. (Remember, some students may never reach **full** inclusion.)

Criteria for full inclusion should be firmly established. See the pages in this book on Individual Assessment and analyze the student again. How much of a transition plan will he or she need? Does the student adjust quickly to change? What portion of his or her behavior program will need to transfer into the regular education classroom? How will the regular education teacher be involved? By having him or her visit for short periods of time? By having the teacher first observe the student in the special education class? Look at the following components:

- What times of day should the transition plan affect?

- How quickly can this transition take place?

- Who will support the student during the transition phase?

Transition plans should always be discussed during the spring IEP to make sure that the student will be adequately prepared for the new teacher in the fall. This can mean visits, desensitization programs, and teacher familiarity. When the students return in the fall, they should be coming into a familiar environment—not an unfamiliar setting!

Academic modifications ("How much of the core curriculum can this student do?")

When an IEP states that academic modifications must be done, this means **you** have to do them! Regular education teachers often believe that they do not have to do academic modifications. However, they are legally required to do them whether they want to or not. This is not a teacher choice!

Responsibility for making these academic modifications, however, can be negotiated between regular education teachers and special education teachers. Be careful; teachers should not place themselves in a position of liability by stating that they will not do them (see Academic Modifications).

Starting and ending times of day ("Whose student is this, anyway??")

When discussing mainstreaming or inclusion programming, ownership of the student should come through regular education personnel, if possible. Ideally, starting and ending each day in the regular education classroom will help the student feel that he or she belongs to that group of students and not be viewed as just another "visitor." What happens in the middle portion of the day depends on the student's needs.

Social skills goals ("Social skills are not part of the core academics!")

Too often, social skills goals are not emphasized in the IEP Process because they are not viewed as part of the core curriculum. **However, for any student with autism, forgetting the social component dismisses 1/3 of their disability!**

Social skills goals are extremely important to our students and are the main reason special education has gone toward inclusive practices for students with autism. Please remember to put social objectives into the IEP! They should be addressed on a **daily** basis, not just once or twice a year when the students attend a school assembly! Both direct and incidental methods should be used. Daily intervention is necessary to help our students generalize the skills to their peers in the school and to their home and community settings.

Behavior plan ("How can I get the student to behave in my class?")

Almost every student with autism will have some form of behavior plan that needs discussion at an IEP meeting. Everyone at the meeting should discuss the philosophy behind the program (whether it is positive or negative). The parents must understand how the student will be encouraged to develop more positive, appropriate behaviors instead of the ones he or she is demonstrating presently. The IEP Team must examine each of the behavioral objectives and make sure that it is encouraging the positive behaviors.

Collaboration between home and school ("How can the parents know that we really are teaching their child?")

IEP meetings can become very rough when there is an adversarial environment. Regular education teachers are rarely prepared for meetings that can sometimes go up to six or eight hours in length (and be stretched out over many months). However, much of the animosity that is sometimes present can be eliminated by prior preparation between the teacher and parents, and by routine, daily correspondence between them both. Working together is extremely important, but both sides must understand the limitations of the other. Everyone at the IEP meeting is striving to do what is best for the student. Trust can be developed between both parties when everyone agrees that there are no real experts in autism and each has to help the other understand this particular child. Only by being able to recognize the gifts that each party brings to the table will the IEP meeting go well.

These are certainly not the only issues to be discussed at an IEP meeting. You will, no doubt, add many more over the years. Neither teachers nor parents should fear an IEP, but should welcome the chance to get together to share ideas, hopes, and dreams for the student.

Keep a long-term mindset as to what the student will need to look like in twenty-five years. This will help everyone focus on how to get him or her there. Good luck! **Remember, flexibility and patience are the most important components at any IEP meeting!**

How Do We Teach
These Students?

Teaching Strategies for Children with Autism

Teaching strategies for children with autism must be individualized. Teaching in the naturalistic setting provides the added benefit of teaching to generalization. Children with autism often have difficulty learning at the same rate and speed that typical children learn, and modifications to the curriculum may need to be made. The following list of interventions may help teachers understand the unique needs of the child with autism in their classroom. Conducting an Individual Analysis will allow the teachers to understand which of these components are suitable for a particular student.

Teaching Interventions for Socialization

- Teach social skills daily with direct and incidental teaching techniques. Curricula available include the *Walker Social Skills Curriculum* by Pro-Ed and *Skillstreaming,* by Research Press (these techniques can be done individually or in groups)

- Make the curricula have an underlying social skills philosophy

- Supervise structured social interactions

- Implement peer tutor programs

- Respect personal space

- Provide "space" to cool down when necessary

- Build in time for teachers to observe the child

- Plan for desensitization to fears

- Reinforce positive social interactions

- Recognize that the child may want to interact but doesn't know how

- Provide specific social rules

- Help the student to change topics when necessary

- Use rehearsal strategies for social situations

- Use our children as peer models in anyway possible

- Seat students in small groups

Teaching Interventions for Communication

- Know each child's abilities
- Teach functional communication skills (**never** give up on the verbal!)
- Plan for independent communication functioning
- Combine communication systems when needed
- Set up opportunities where the child **must** communicate
- Reinforce communication
- Use appropriate language for the child (short-sentence structure)
- Use concrete language (eliminate abstract concepts)
- Demonstrate nonverbal communication (use gestures with speech)
- Teach specific functional gestures
- Determine communicative attempts exhibited by behavior

Teaching Interventions for Restricted Repertoire of Activities

- Analyze environment for distracting objects and activities
- Control environmental stimuli as much as possible
- Prepare and explain changes in routine
- Teach and reinforce new activities
- Teach choice
- Teach concrete appropriate behaviors to replace inappropriate behaviors. (Don't expect inappropriate behaviors to just disappear!)
- Start with small intervals of time and reinforce appropriate behaviors. Build on success!
- Use self-stimulatory acts as temporary reinforcers—if possible
- Fade self-stimulatory behaviors in favor of appropriate activities
- Use age-appropriate materials

General Teaching Interventions

- Know your expectations

- Present realistic expectations to the children and teach to increase independent skills

- Analyze individual strengths and weaknesses (do not assume all students with autism will have the same strengths and weaknesses.)

- Teach skills where they will be used; in natural situations and across all settings

- Use demonstration, modeling, and shaping to teach skills

- Provide consistent, visual schedules of the daily events posted on the wall. May need to individualize these

- Vary teaching formats (large group, small group, and one-on-one)

- Expect to gather the child's attention

- Work to maintain eye contact

- Allow short breaks between teaching sessions

- Pair a preferred activity with a non-preferred activity

- Be consistent

- Use positive behavior programming

- Provide time to be alone, if needed

- Include regular exercise

- Review reinforcers periodically and conduct motivational surveys

- Be aware of any medical needs. (Know and understand medications the student is on and provide updates to doctors, if needed.)

- Have frequent contact with parents

- Understand that children with autism vary in characteristics and abilities

Paraprofessional Support for Students with Autism in Inclusive Settings

Many components are necessary to ensure the success of an inclusion program for students with autism. Among those are paraprofessionals, who play an essential role in inclusive regular education classrooms.

Paraprofessionals are assigned to students to provide extra support during the times deemed necessary by the student's IEP. However, in inclusive settings, the paraprofessional's job is often poorly defined. The paraprofessional may have several different duties: support in full-time regular education, part-time regular education, full-time special education, or part-time special education. Teachers and paraprofessionals alike should consider the following issues when designing a support system in the regular education setting for a student with autism.

Teachers need to supervise paraprofessionals. This supervision can be provided by the regular education teacher, special education teacher, or inclusion coordinator. Weekly meetings should review IEP goals and objectives, data collection, behavioral and social programming, transitions, and modifications to academics.

Paraprofessionals are crucial to the success of the program, and, as a result, they often know the student the most intimately. However, all paraprofessionals, even those that are the most familiar with the needs of the student, need supervision. Paraprofessionals should not be expected to shoulder the same responsibility load as the teacher. Despite the difference in supervisory responsibility, teachers and paraprofessionals should still collaborate on teaching. Collaborative teaching between the teacher and the paraprofessional can take different forms:

- Small group instruction (teacher and paraprofessional split the class)

- Teacher and paraprofessional switching roles during a lesson (paraprofessional leads the class while teacher is responsible for target students)

The paraprofessional should follow the academic modifications made by the teachers. He or she can contribute to this effort by relaying progress to special and regular education teachers. In some circumstances,

the paraprofessional can be responsible for making the curriculum adaptations (reducing the number of problems thus giving the student more time), but the paraprofessional must be supervised by the regular or special education teacher.

The paraprofessional should make sure that the daily peer programs are conducted (by the teacher or the paraprofessional). The paraprofessional should ensure that "friends" or "buddies of the day" have been chosen, that two or three marbles are given out each day (see *Marble Jar* program), and other social programs are being conducted. Also, the paraprofessional should set up interactions between the student and peers whenever possible. Setting up interactions with other students can be accomplished through some of the following actions.

- Place the student in proximity of other children

- Let the student watch other children

- Encourage the student to ask questions ("Can I play?; or, "Can you help me?")

- Have the student participate in the activity

- Encourage the child to share materials with other students

The paraprofessional should become very familiar with the student's behavior plan and consistently use it. The paraprofessional plays an important part in ensuring that the plan is being consistently implemented during the times when he or she is not with the student. The paraprofessional must ensure that the student has time to receive any reward that he or she has earned with the plan. In addition, the paraprofessional has to review behavioral or academic data to monitor the student's progress.

The student's IEP sets the goals and objectives. This means that the paraprofessional's data collection needs to be monitored by the special education teacher, because this will be the method used to assess individual objectives and goals. It is appropriate (and suggested) for the paraprofessional to set his or her own personal goals for the student (goals that he or she can teach, monitor, and track). This will help the paraprofessional take ownership in the student and form a solid relationship.

Although the paraprofessional may have other responsibilities in the classroom, it is important for him or her to continually know what is happening with the target student and assess where the student needs help. Questions to consider:

- What is the student doing?

- Is the student isolated?

- Is the work at his or her level?

- Is the student being taken advantage of by other students?

- Is the student occupied with self-stim behavior? Does he or she need direction from me? If the student needs help, can the direction or cue be better provided by a peer?

There should not be a time when the paraprofessional has nothing to do. He or she should take the initiative to find something to do that can help: first, for the student; second, for the other students; and third for the teacher.

The paraprofessional must be familiar with the room. The paraprofessional must be able to find all material easily so that he or she is not constantly looking for basic materials. This prevents disruption. Also, the paraprofessional should work quietly in the room, and talking or prompting should not interrupt the teaching lesson. The paraprofessional must follow the lead of the regular education teacher. If the teacher changes the schedule, the paraprofessional has to be prepared to provide support to the student.

The paraprofessional may or may not be on the student's IEP team. The paraprofessional should attend the IEP meetings, if possible, because he or she will have the best idea of the student's current level of functioning. If the paraprofessional is unable to attend the meetings, he or she should write a statement outlining the student's strengths and weaknesses to the IEP team. The paraprofessional needs to be familiar with the student's IEP goals and objectives. He or she needs to keep these goals in mind while working with the student.

The paraprofessional is responsible for keeping the correspondence between home and school running smoothly. He or she should remember to check the student's backpack every morning for messages from home, and then write daily in the journal (if the teacher wishes) to inform the parents of successes and areas of difficulty. It is important to highlight some positive behaviors in the journal, but you should also include challenges that have occurred. Remember, because of legal issues, the teacher **must** review what the paraprofessional has written and then sign the journal. The teacher must assume all legal responsibility in his or her classroom.

Paraprofessionals should not pull the student out of the regular education environment for academics without clearing it first with special education (remember the IEP!). By law, the student must fulfill the terms of the IEP. Paraprofessionals should not be placed in positions of liability by changing these terms on their own.

A paraprofessional's job is not easy, especially with a student with autism. However, it is important for the paraprofessional to remain as positive as possible, even when frustrated. He or she should refrain from using "negatives" ("No," "Don't do that," "Stop that," etc.)

The paraprofessional should tell the student what he or she wants the student to do in place of the inappropriate behavior.

Our students often become overly sensitive to the frequent use of negative terms, and behaviors can dramatically increase when they are always told, "No." Although it is difficult to eliminate negative terms from a teacher's or paraprofessional's repertoire, catching each other and reminding each other about not using particular words can help to eliminate them. Save the stern "No!" for times when the student is in a dangerous situation and **must stop immediately.** At these times, you just want compliance, not new skills!

There are many issues to consider when planning for paraprofessional support in an inclusion program. Some issues that may prevent paraprofessionals from being effective members of an inclusion team include:

- Lack of training

- Assignment to other duties (lunch duty, making copies, running errands, etc.), which make them absent from their inclusion duties

- Lack of supervision

Nevertheless, a dedicated paraprofessional can have a tremendous impact on a student's progress in regular education and in life.

Academic Modifications for Inclusion

Most students with autism do not learn the same as typical students. Even those students who have demonstrated average (or high) cognitive abilities often have difficulty with the regular education curriculum. Although resource classrooms offer intensive, individualized instruction in certain content areas, they are often not sufficient substitutes for instruction in the regular education classroom. Therefore, it is often necessary for the regular education teacher to make changes to the curriculum to help the student with autism succeed. Academic modifications can take on many forms, as outlined below.

Modification of Activities and Materials

There are many ways to modify activities and materials to meet the needs of the student. Numerous textbooks have outlined ways in which to explore doing it. One such book, *Adapting Curriculum and Instruction in Inclusive Classrooms: A Teacher's Desk Reference* (Deschenes, Ebeling, and Sprague, ISDD, 1994) offers an excellent guide to adapting curricula in the regular education classroom. It is extremely teacher-friendly and easy to implement.

Judy Wood's *Adapting Instruction to Accommodate Students in Inclusive Settings* should also be explored. The following adaption strategies are a collection of suggestions from these books, as well as other materials that we have collected over the years. (Most are from the Deschenes, Ebeling & Sprague book, however).

Size

Adjust the number of items that the student must learn or complete; e.g., require the student to complete only the odd numbers on the math assignment.

Time

Adjust the time allotted for learning, completing assignments, testing, etc. Let the student continue working on an assignment while the rest of the classmates move on to a new lesson.

Level of Support

Increase the level of support that the student receives during a lesson or assignment. For example, have an aide work with the student, or assign peer buddies, peer tutors, or cross-age tutors.

Input

Adapt the way the instruction is delivered to the student (e.g., allow the student to take home a copy of the teacher's notes from the lesson).

Output

Allow the student to respond to the instruction in a different way; you could allow the student to type responses or answer questions verbally.

Difficulty

Adjust the level of difficulty of the material being presented or the work that the student must complete; for example, let the student use a calculator when solving math problems.

Participation

Adjust the level of participation in the task that the student is doing; for example, during a group reading lesson, have the student turn the pages of the book.

Alternate Goals

Have different goals for the student to meet using the same materials—you can have the student work on identifying sight words while the rest of the students are looking up the definitions in the dictionary.

Substitute Curriculum

Use different instruction and materials to meet the student's individual goals. You can let the student work on computer skills while the rest of the class is learning long division.

Modification of Instruction

Another way to address the academic needs of a student with autism is to modify the way the instruction of the material is presented. Many teachers do this instinctively, without realizing it, in order to address the needs of all their students. No **one** teaching method is best for all students with autism. However, students tend to respond best to strategies that are more concrete, that allow many opportunities to practice the skill across different activities and settings, and grant the opportunities to observe and interact with peers.

Teachers must examine their methods to ensure that they are not using abstract concepts that might confuse the student (e.g., "a few problems...," "a selection of these...," "when you are ready...," and so on).

Teaching Format

Varying teaching formats across the day allows the student to develop different learning strategies. Examples of these:

- Lecture/Demonstration/Practice
- Hands-on Demonstration
- Experiential Learning
- Cooperative Learning
- One-on-One

Instructional Grouping

Altering the instructional grouping provides students with different situations in which to learn and practice new skills. Make sure the student has a selection of the list below, but assign the selection during the appropriate academic times to allow for the student's strengths and weaknesses. For example, assigning group time might be better for one student during math rather than during reading time, because it involves more manipulatives (a strength for this particular student). Groupings include:

- Whole Group
- Small Group
- Peer Buddies
- Individual

Rate of Instruction

A limited attention span hinders academic times. Therefore, after gauging the average attention span for your student, you can use several of the following strategies within the context of the academic sessions.

- Stop periodically to ascertain student comprehension
- Intersperse small breaks
- Allow students to work at own rate

Alternative Approaches

Although it is often difficult to run separate curricula within the context of the general education classroom, these can be incorporated with the regular curriculum by:

- Using non-standard curriculum approaches (whole language, sight-word reading, etc.)
- Using alternate forms of communication (pictures, signs, etc.)

Setting

Most students periodically enjoy a change of setting. This helps students refocus their attention by receiving a small break on the way to the new location.

- Give instruction in an applied setting (teach alphabetization skills in the library with books, teach science lessons on plants in the school garden, etc.)
- Give instruction in different environments (provide a change in noise level, distractions, climate, etc.)

Modification of Environment

You may have to alter the environment for a student with autism so that he or she can learn successfully in regular education. The environment is not just the classroom setting; it also includes any additional materials, rules, or privileges that are not typically a part of the daily classroom routine.

Behavioral Arrangement

- Behavior plans
- Self-management (daily planner, checklists, timer, etc.)
- Study skills (outlines, written steps, lists, etc.)
- Visual schedules (daily, activity-based, etc.).

Physical Arrangement

- Desk placement
- Materials placement

- Quiet zone

- Study carrel

Sensory Arrangement

- Sensory materials (stress ball, Walkman, bean bags, etc.)

- Sensory-blocking materials (ear plugs, flicker-blocking lenses, etc.)

- Assistive devices

Important Considerations

There are several important points to take into consideration when making modifications to a student's curriculum. In order for a modified curriculum to be effective, it should:

- Use least intrusive methods

  Modifications should not separate the student from the lesson or activity. Employ least intrusive methods first. Use more intrusive methods only when the less intrusive ones do not work.

- Be teacher-friendly

  If the modifications are too complicated (or take too much teacher time), the teacher will probably not consistently use them. Modifications should work well with the regular education teacher's lesson plan. They require a reasonable amount of additional teacher planning time.

- Be economically practical

  Certain assistive devices that are currently available (DragonSpeak, CheapTalk, portable computer, etc.) may provide students with opportunities to participate more fully with their typical peers. However, these devices can be very expensive. You must assess whether modifications are economically practical for the school and the student's family, and whether you could use alternatives.

  Many electronic communication devices are extremely fragile and will not survive being tossed across the room. Repair time can take many months. Make sure you investigate your choice thoroughly!

- Teach necessary skills

  All modifications should aim at teaching the student necessary skills that he or she will need when growing older. It is important not to eliminate all educational obstacles to the point that the student does not learn how to problem-solve the skills necessary to function in the real world.

- Allow for social interaction

  An adapted curriculum should allow the student as much opportunity for social interaction as possible. This is the reason he or she is in regular education!

- Use a functional curriculum

  The student's IEP contains both functional and academic goals and objectives that the student needs to learn. Both areas need to be addressed in the general education classroom. As the student ages, the functional goals can become more difficult to implement in the general education classroom setting without placing the student in the position of being singled out.

- Provide for generalization of skills

  Students with autism have great difficulty with generalizing skills across different environments and situations. Any modified curriculum should provide opportunities to generalize the new skills. This may mean that the student needs to use the skills in meaningful situations, or that the skills need to be taught in the places where they are meant to be used.

Further Considerations

The student's IEP should be the guiding force behind all curriculum adaptations. The IEP should indicate what type of adaptations are necessary and who will make the changes (regular education or special education teacher, paraprofessional, speech teacher, occupational therapist, etc.).

The student's IEP should also indicate how the modified curricula should be graded. If the IEP does not outline a grading system, the teacher must consider how he or she will grade the student. Many teachers feel uncomfortable grading a student with autism on the same scale as typical students. For this reason, a modified report card may be appropriate. However, if the teacher finds he or she is making adaptations without guidelines in the IEP, the teacher can decide whether changes require a modified grading system or report card.

Technically, any modifications made to the normal curriculum because of a student's disability qualify as curriculum adaptations. However, many teachers feel that some simple modifications, such as allowing the student to type rather than handwrite a report, are not sufficient to require a modified grading system. Unless specified by the IEP, the teacher has the right to decide what material to modify, how to do it, and how to grade it. If the teacher feels that his or her modifications are significant enough to warrant a separate grading system, he or she can indicate "modified" on the student's report card next to the subject that has been modified.

Students who have had curriculum adaptations all the way through school can still graduate from high school with a diploma. However, students need to pass the "Graduation Exam" to receive a "College Track" diploma. This test **cannot** be modified as outlined under current legislation. This legislation will go through changes in 2000, so it is best for teachers and parents to become familiar with the grading system. If the student has the skills necessary to continue in post-secondary education, teachers and parents must consider whether academic modifications will adequately prepare the student to pass the Graduation Exam. If not, the student may need additional tutoring in the general education curriculum. As a rule, it is best to modify curricula only when absolutely necessary for the student to learn and progress in the regular education environment.

Data Collection

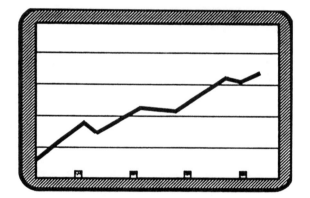

Taking Data in Inclusive Settings

Why Does It Have to Be Done?

Special education teachers usually have a lot of experience collecting academic, social, and behavioral data on their students. However, regular education teachers and paraprofessionals often become overwhelmed when told that they need to take individualized data on a student in their class, on themselves, or on another teacher.

Data collection can appear time-consuming and confusing to someone who is not used to doing it and who does not understand why the data is needed. Taking data in the regular education classroom, however, is an important part of any inclusion project and needs to be mastered (and appreciated!) by regular and special education teachers, staff, etc.

An important aspect of teaching involves assessing what the students have learned. This involves grading assignments and giving tests. These methods give the teacher a very good picture of what students have learned academically, but they do not address other areas that need to be tracked, such as social goals, initiations and responses, or numbers of social bids. The main purpose of inclusion is to give the student with autism opportunities to learn appropriate language, behavior, and, most importantly, social skills. To discover whether or not the student is learning these skills, the teacher (or paraprofessional) will need to take data on these areas. This helps the teacher obtain a picture of how the student is progressing toward **all** goals. This data is often an excellent reflection of all the hard work that the teacher has been doing.

Teachers are usually assessed on their personal teaching ability through traditional methods (student achievement scores, principal observation, etc.). These assessments often do not adequately measure many of the skills needed to work in an inclusive setting. For this reason, all teachers (regular education, special education, and support personnel) need to continually assess their own abilities as they relate to working with a special needs student.

Several forms are provided in the Appendix. Inclusion coordinators often find these forms helpful in teaching, targeting specific goals, and assessing inclusion personnel. These forms can also be kept throughout the school year to show overall changes, and they can be an excellent method to boost self-esteem when changes are seen. Other forms are also provided in the Appendix that can help the teacher determine the function of a particular behavior and show which items will most likely reinforce positive behaviors. Information gained from these forms can provide the teacher with new insight into teaching strategies for students with autism. Although data collection may seem like a lot of work up-front, it actually prevents more work in the future!

Weekly Data Tracking

Collecting data on a daily basis assists inclusion teachers in tracking a student's progress over time, which allows for adjustment in the educational program. The *Weekly Tracking Form* (found in the Appendix) has been designed to highlight behavioral changes and allows for easy interpretation of the results. This form does not substitute for routine data tracking on individual goals and objectives, but it supplements routine data tracking for the purposes of noting social, behavioral, and communication changes in the generalized setting.

The form should be completed each day by an adult who is familiar with the student with autism. A paraprofessional, inclusion coordinator, special or regular education teacher, etc., can complete the form. While it is not necessary for the same person to take data each day, consistency in data collection is important. Data is collected in a regular education classroom to better judge generalizing effects.

A copy of the data form can be sent home with the student at the end of each week to provide parents with information on their child's progress. A copy of this form should also be kept by the student's teacher or inclusion coordinator so that data can be compared throughout the year and used to modify IEP goals. Instructions on completing the form are outlined below.

Language sample

For children with expressive language delays or difficulties in pragmatics, language data should be taken (ideally) once or twice a day during free time (recess) or a language-based activity. The observer should document a selection of language (alternative forms of communication, if appropriate) that the targeted student uses during a ten-minute interval. The observer should also check "S" or "P" to indicate whether each communication attempt is "Spontaneous" or "Prompted." Try to record as many instances of verbal speech as the form allows. Over time, you will be able to see progress, or lack of it.

Initiations

Ideally, initiation data should be taken once a day during recess or other unstructured social time for a ten-minute interval. (The bare minimum would be three times per week). The observer should indicate the number of initiation attempts that the target student makes toward peers. For each attempt, the observer should slash a number on the chart, starting at one. At the end of the week, the highest number of initiations slashed for each day can be connected by a line to form a simple graph for quick interpretation of results.

Activity level

For students who have high activity levels, and for students who are on medication trials, the observer should document the overall activity level of the target student each day. If the student is not in regular education for the entire day, the time that the data is collected should be indicated under "time." The results can also be connected to form a graph. An "AM" and "PM" column are provided for greater specificity.

Inappropriate behaviors

For students who have significant behavior problems, the teacher can use the form for simple event recording. The form can be the first step in a functional analysis. Activities that prove difficult for the student should be targeted for the data recording in order to see the intensity of the particular behavior. High levels of behavior should then receive further analysis and accompanying positive behavior programs (DRO systems can then be applied).

The form in the Appendix of this book allows space for three different behaviors. The same behaviors can be tracked each week, but they may change with the student's progress. If the student is using the *Rocket Ship* program, the three behaviors should reflect the three rules on the plan.

Successful completion of behavior plan

Each day, the observer should document successful completion of the student's behavior plan (*Rocket Ship, Flower Chart, Snake Race, Puzzle Piece,* other individualized plans, or the class-wide behavior management system) by checking the box. This helps the teacher to quickly gain the information regarding total weekly progress.

Data tracking is usually the last thing that teachers want to do, but it can be the most important component of any program for a student with special needs. Many teachers have had to defend their program and teaching style in lawsuits. Without data to substantiate methods, the teacher can be in trouble! Teachers should devise a data tracking system that best suits his or her needs, but that contains everything that the various teachers have to have to monitor and modify the student's program.

A Note about Middle School

Transition Planning for Middle School

Many parents and teachers worry about our students with autism when they are about to transition to middle school. With good reason! Who was it that thought we should present the most chaotic form of educational structure to students during the most chaotic time of their lives?

Middle school students will usually have anywhere from five to six different teachers in one day; the entire day's schedules can be flipped on a daily or weekly basis, and no one really takes ownership of anyone! This leads to all sorts of troubles for a student with autism. There are some ways to get around this system, but it will take work, concentrated consistency on everyone's part, and the dedication of the special education teacher to make sure that all of the bases are covered with the student with autism. The following suggestions are offered to teachers and parents in hope that you will find some of them helpful. However, middle school has no guarantees!

Step One

In the spring, during 5th grade, the special education teacher should contact the special education teacher in the middle school to discuss the program. She or he should be asked questions regarding inclusion methods, behavioral practices, and motivational strategies. Also, the teacher must inquire about any peer programming that is already being conducted.

What are the levels of paraprofessional/support personnel? What are their skill levels? How supportive is the administration toward innovative practices? Do they ever come and observe your students? Does the teacher have a good grounding in positive behavioral methods? How long has the teacher been teaching? Do you get the impression that he or she is about "burned-out?"

How do the teacher's present students handle all the changes that occur during the day? Has the teacher assigned "hall buddies" for any students? What is the level of coordination between the teacher and the general education teachers?

What about the parents? Does the teacher send journals home each night? How often does the teacher meet with the parents to just discuss progress (not just "crisis" meetings)? Are there are any after-school activities that your student might be interested in joining? More importantly, how often does the entire daily schedule change?

Step Two

A meeting should call the relevant teachers of both the elementary and middle school so that they can meet with the parents and student and discuss the child entering the middle school next fall. Discuss every topic. Write down questions or topics ahead of time so that everyone remembers them and is then able to gain as much knowledge about this impending transition as possible.

Step Three

If possible, the student should go to the middle school in progressively longer time spans to "experience" a day in the new school. Usually, the special education teacher does this, but parents may wish to as well. Peer buddies should be chosen ahead of time by the middle school representative so that these students can accompany the new student around the halls. Depending on the reactions of the new student, this "desensitization process" can go as quickly or as slowly as necessary. However, the student should experience as much of a full day as possible, including transition times (with hundreds of students changing classes), the bells ringing, lunchtime noises, full-period classes, etc. This will be to the student's benefit.

Step Four

The student's homeroom teacher should be chosen during the spring term before the student enters middle school. This teacher should be as familiar as possible with the new student and be the person to "claim" the new student. The teacher has to take ownership of the student for coordination purposes with the special education teacher, unless another classroom teacher is identified. Sometimes the homeroom teacher sees the student a few minutes, whereas another teacher may have the student for several periods each day. In that case, whoever has the student the most, should claim ownership.

Step Five

The student with autism must learn emergency plans ahead of time. For example, the student should receive reassurance that if he or she is lost in the school, loses books, or has any other "emergency," he or she is to come directly to one particular area (probably the special education room).

The unknown frustrates and frightens our students. In the past, a middle school student has run down the hallway crying when he left his books in one room and had to move onto another class. Simple emergency plans can help to alleviate the very real fear that our students can experience when faced with new situations.

Step Six

As soon as school starts in the fall, the special education teacher should set up peer programs, or "hall buddies," that consist of students (possibly 7th or 8th graders) that can watch out for the new student and help direct him or her. It is always better for the new student if someone will help him or her in those first few weeks of school. Caution should be noted, however, in the selection of peer buddies, as middle school students can be very immature and do not always prove to be the best models!

Step Seven

Since daily schedules change often and rapidly, visual systems take on an added importance. A written schedule is absolutely crucial to the functioning of the new student. Please remember that our students are visual learners and are not usually auditory learners! Write the schedules down on cards or notepaper and have the new student carry this around with him or her in a folder or backpack. The student can refer to the schedules throughout the day until he or she becomes comfortable. However, the teacher needs to be aware of impending changes in the schedule to update the visual chart to prepare the student for the new system.

Step Eight

Continual analysis of the middle school schedules and ownership by one teacher are the only hopes for preparing students to survive in this chaotic environment! Please remember this aspect when you start thinking about the transition process into middle school for inclusive students with autism. We wish you the best of luck luck!

Partnership
between Home and School

Collaboration between Home and School

Without It, Can Inclusion Truly Work?

Ultimately, a major component to realizing the dream of inclusion is the dedicated collaboration between home and school. This helps to ensure the generalization of the skills taught in both settings. However, generalization of skills can be extremely difficult for individuals with autism. They need opportunities to practice their skills in as natural a setting as possible in order to "generalize" what they have learned. This is the reason we look toward regular education classes for our students and work to provide inclusive settings.

The goal of generalization of skills, however, can be hampered unless teachers truly coordinate objectives and strategies with a child's parents. Methods to enhance this goal can be to offer opportunities for observation in the classroom, consider the home setting and conditions before writing behavior plans, ask for parents' opinions and their dreams for their child, plan and conduct parent training to increase consistency of the application of behavior plans, etc.

Parents have the right to expect (and should ask for) a "cross-training," generalization program among all teachers and the home. Parents' dreams regarding their child are usually for as much inclusion into their community as possible, and the lack of collaboration will hinder this goal. Students can gain the needed generalization of skills through continual collaboration between all parties working with them. Periodic meetings, utilizing part of the student's "related services" time set aside for in-class treatment or teacher training, behavior plans that cross all settings, daily journals between home and school, etc., can all work toward this goal. Generalization cannot occur in isolated settings with isolated people! Students with autism deserve to have consistent programs that cross all boundaries and settings. In this way, inclusion can truly work!

A Parent's Perspective of Inclusion

Participating in the Emory School-Age Inclusion Project

"Regular education classes are like a foreign country to us. For two years, it was our dream to live in this country. We researched it, studied it, talked to people who lived there, and even made brief visits ourselves. But we couldn't get our resident visas until we were invited to participate in the Emory Autism Inclusion Project. "

"As we'd always feared, the move has not been easy. The natives speak a foreign language, so communicating is difficult. They also engage in all sorts of strange and meaningless rituals, which can be intensely frustrating. For the first time, we realize how "different" we are, and that hurts."

"But the best environment in which to learn a foreign language is to be immersed in it as a child. And it's working! We're starting to learn, and even enjoy, some of this strange language. We're interested in friends and how to make them. We're picking up typical slang expressions and experimenting with telling jokes. We're even recognizing and responding appropriately to the feelings of others. And the natives have learned that even though we're "different," we're smart, loveable, and have our own special abilities to offer."

"We're very grateful to the Inclusion Project for making our move possible. Without support and some "interpreting," it might never have happened. But thanks to this initiative, we're exactly where we need to be - and we hope to stay there!"

C. Wilkerson
Parent

Contributions

Turkey Hand

by Erik W., an eight-year-old student with Asperger's Syndrome

From the Students

What would inclusion be without the students? Some of the little artists in the EARC Inclusion Project allowed us to include their work in this book. Thanks to them, all the hard work is worth it!

All About Me in a Video

Hi, my name is Erik and this is a video about the things I like to do. My favorite things are making electric circuits and reading books. My favorite book is "1001 Questions and Answers World of Knowledge" because when I read it, I learn about science and technology. I also like to read stories about animals and adventures. Some of my other favorite books are "Peter Pan" and "Hercules" and "Charlotte's Web."

I like to work on my computer. I like to play Compact Disc games. I like to play "Gizmos and Gadgets" and "Outnumbered" and "Myst." My favorite games is "Gizmos and Gadgets." You try to beat Morty, the Master of Mischief, by beating him in all fiftenn races. You have to find the best parts of the vehicles and build the behicles and race with thyem against Morty. I became Head Scientist by beating Morty in all fifteen races.

I like to play music on the piano and I like to sing. I like to play piano pieces by Mozart, Beethoven, and Dvorak. I played the piano in the Talent Show at my school. I played the "Turkish March" by Ludwig Von Beethoven and the "Finale" of the "new Wold Symphony" by Antonin Dvorak. Someday I want to play the saxophone, the recorder, and the Suzaphone. It is the large instrument that looks like a boa constrictor with a wide open mouth. I like to make up my own pieces on the piano too. I like to put in chords and sharps and flats and regular notes.

Erik T.

If I Had a Dog

If I had a dog I would play with him and feed him too. I would even give him something to play with like a ball. I would take him for walks in the woods and down by the lake. I would take him in the water with me and we would take toys which could hold water like a paddle swirl with two paddle swirl water holders. If I had a dog I would let him sleep in a basket with a sheet that keeps dog hair off the basket. When he wakes up in the middle of the night and he would cry because he is hungry I would feed him dog food in his bowl and when he ate it he wouldn't cry anymore. I would name my dog Furry because he would be a furry dog.

by Erik T., a 6-year-old student with Asperger's Syndrome

Fred and Barney

by Sam K., an 8 year-old student with autism

The Case Kids

Matt and Sandy were in the Boy bathroom on the 3rd grade hall. They found a word written on the wall. "What does it mean?" asked Matt. "Its too nasty to tell you." said Sandy. The next day, another nasty word was on the wall of the bathroom. There was also a spitball on the ceiling. "All right, that's it, that tears it!" said Sandy. Matt told the principal about it. He said he would clean it up. When Matt and Sandy went in the bathroom they saw another sentence on the wall that said I LOVE ASHLEY. Zach got very upset. The principal cleaned every word, all but I LOVE ASHLEY. The next day there was ANOTHER BAD WORD ON THE WALL!!! At lunch, Matt had an idea. The idea was agreed. Matt, Sandy, Zach and a few more kids became a crime busting club called The Case Kids.

by Matt W., an eight-year-old student with Asperger's Syndrome

Notes from an "AS" to an NT

The following story was written by Mary Margaret, an adult with Asperger's Syndrome, for all of us labeled as "Neurotypicals" in the hope that we will come to understand a little about this disorder.

Getting Acclimated

I think my mama is from Mars
and my daddy is from Pluto.
My sister is an Eskimo
and my brother is a spy.
I hope I am right
because
I don't seem to fit in this earth skin.
Sometimes I think there must
be a planet or a country
with people like me,
people who aren't from this place.
I don't seem to understand
the language of the natives
and my parents aren't helping me.
Why don't I fit,
why don't I belong?
I wish I could fly away to my real home
but I am afraid of heights.
And I wish I could burrow under the ground
and go all the way to China
but I am afraid of small spaces.
I wish I could tell the world
who I really am
but I am afraid of
the earthings.
What if I never acclimate
to their weather, their customs, their crowds?
Will I die alone
in the skin that doesn't fit?
I am so tired of this mission.
When do I get to go home?
I watch Boo Radley and I know he knows how to get there.
I watch Starman and he makes it looks so easy.
I watch Martin Luther King and he talks of being free.
Does anyone watch me?

A Final Word

Throughout any inclusion project, there will be many tears: tears of frustration and tears of joy. When things are difficult, just remember the impact you are making on these young people's lives. Without opportunities for inclusion, their options in this world would be sadly limited.

Inclusion programming, when done correctly and designed for success, can be extremely rewarding for all individuals involved. With the dedication and enthusiasm of teachers and parents working together, this goal can be achieved!

Appendix

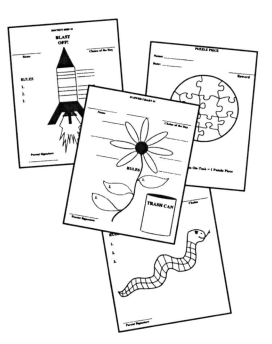

Weekly Data Tracking Form

Student Name: Week of: Completed by:

10-Minute Language Sample

M		Tu		W			Th		F		
Time:		Time:		Time:			Time:		Time:		
Activity:		Activity:		Activity:			Activity:		Activity:		
Language:	S	Language:	S	Language:	S	P	Language:	S	Language:	S	P

Initiations (10-minute sample)

M	Tu	W	Th	F
Time:	Time:	Time:	Time:	Time:
10	10	10	10	10
9	9	9	9	9
8	8	8	8	8
7	7	7	7	7
6	6	6	6	6
5	5	5	5	5
4	4	4	4	4
3	3	3	3	3
2	2	2	2	2
1	1	1	1	1
0	0	0	0	0

Activity Level

M	Tu	W	Th	F
AM	AM	AM	AM	AM
High	High	High	High	High
Average	Average	Average	Average	Average
Low	Low	Low	Low	Low
PM	PM	PM	PM	PM
High	High	High	High	High
Average	Average	Average	Average	Average
Low	Low	Low	Low	Low

Inappropriate Behaviors

			Behavior #1	Behavior #2	Behavior #3
M	Time:	Activity:	0 1 2 3 4 5 6 7 8 9 10	0 1 2 3 4 5 6 7 8 9 10	0 1 2 3 4 5 6 7 8 9 10
Tu	Time:	Activity:	0 1 2 3 4 5 6 7 8 9 10	0 1 2 3 4 5 6 7 8 9 10	0 1 2 3 4 5 6 7 8 9 10
W	Time:	Activity:	0 1 2 3 4 5 6 7 8 9 10	0 1 2 3 4 5 6 7 8 9 10	0 1 2 3 4 5 6 7 8 9 10
Th	Time:	Activity:	0 1 2 3 4 5 6 7 8 9 10	0 1 2 3 4 5 6 7 8 9 10	0 1 2 3 4 5 6 7 8 9 10
F	Time:	Activity:	0 1 2 3 4 5 6 7 8 9 10	0 1 2 3 4 5 6 7 8 9 10	0 1 2 3 4 5 6 7 8 9 10

Comments:

Successful Completion of Behavior Plan

M	Tu	W	Th	F

Data Collection in an Inclusive Setting

Student_____ Beginning Date_____

Objective	M	Tu	W	Th	F

Student_____ Beginning Date_____

Objective	M	Tu	W	Th	F

Student_____ Beginning Date_____

Objective	M	Tu	W	Th	F

** Record data <u>at least three times a week</u> on each objective.

Academic/Behavior Checklist

Regular Education Teacher

This form is generally used for supervision/quality control of a new teacher of inclusive strategies. Diplomacy must be used when providing feedback to maintain the enthusiasm.

Teacher_____

Score +, 0, or NA   Criterion: + or NA on all items in 30-minute interval.

Did the Teacher:	Obs. Date		Obs. Date		Obs. Date	
1. Use peers in teaching?						
2. Use reinforcements?						
3. Use redirection through prompting and peer interaction?						
4. Capitalize on teachable moments to teach social skills?						
5. Praise peers for working with buddy?						
6. Set expectations at the beginning of each teaching session?						
7. Teach social skills with direct instruction?						
8. Is the student sitting in appropriate seat?						
9. Is the peer buddy visible and clearly seen by all?						
10. Is the behavior chart and daily schedule posted in the room visible to the child?						
11. Is the peer buddy utilized to the fullest measure?						

Comments:

Academic/Behavior Checklist

Paraprofessional

This form is used to aid in quality control of paraprofessional support techniques.

Paraprofessional_____   Classroom_____

Score +, 0, or NA   Criterion: + or NA on all items in 30 min. interval.

Did the Paraprofessional:	Obs. Date		Obs. Date		Obs. Date	
1. Contact the student?						
2. Orchestrate peer contacts?						
3. Use positive methods to direct?						
4. Provide reinforcement?						
5. Review the schedule?						
6. Adequately handle behavior problems?						
7. Promote peer involvement? How many times?						
8. Use appropriate vocal tone (positive)?						
9. Attempt to build independent working skills? How?						
10. Follow teacher's lead on academics?						
11. Run social skills groups this week?						
12. Teach social objectives incidentally? How?						
13. Analyze situations adequately?						
14. Remain proactive in situations?						

Comments:

Academic/Behavior Checklist

Special Education Teacher

This form can be used to assess the quality of the strategies and methods utilized by the special education teacher. It can provide much information for a feedback session.

Teacher_____

Score +, 0, or NA   Criterion: + or NA on all items in 30 min. interval.

Did the Teacher:	Obs. Date		Obs. Date		Obs. Date	
1. Adequately supervise support staff?						
2. Provide sufficient explanation and demonstration?						
3. Analyze situations adequately?						
4. Provide appropriate suggestions to the regular education teacher and support staff?						
5. How much contact time did the teacher have with each student?						
6. How much contact time did the teacher have with the paraprofessionals?						

Comments:

Teacher Self-check

Example

This form can be used by any member of the inclusion teaching staff to check his or her implementation of inclusive teaching strategies throughout the week. The following form offers an example of possible teaching goals.

Name:_____ Week of:_____

Student:_____

Activity/Teaching Task	Mon.	Tues.	Wed.	Thurs	Fri
Small Group Instruction-taught sharing/turn-taking					
Social Skills Group-5 min to group					
Met/Instruction given to paraprofessional					
Taught choice					
Used Errorless learning					
Used Positive Behavior Plan					
Used random turn-taking					
Varied motivators					
Taught through a peer					
Met with regular education teacher					
Taught social skills incidentally					
Assigned class manager role					
Implemented Friends Club					
Took 5 minutes of time sampling					
Pressed for responsive smile					

TEACHER SELF-CHECK

This form can be used by any member of the inclusion teaching staff to check his or her implementation of inclusive teaching strategies throughout the week.

Name: _____ Week of:_____

Student:_____

Activity/Teaching Task	Mon.	Tues.	Wed.	Thurs.	Fri.

Functional Analysis of Behavior

Student:

Date & Time	People Involved/Activity	Description of Behavior	Duration	Antecedent Circumstances	Consequent Responses from Others

Classroom Motivator Assessment

Student name: _____ Date: _____

Teacher: _____ Grade: _____

Person completing form: _____

The items listed in this assessment are to be used as a guideline for the motivator assessment. School classrooms often have many other items that can be used as motivators for individual students. Additional lines are added for your convenience. Items checked off in the "Very Rewarding" and "Somewhat Rewarding" columns are indicative of rewards that can be used as motivators in school programming.

Item	Very Rewarding	Somewhat Rewarding	Not Rewarding
Praise			
Computer time			
Stickers			
Awards			
Smiley faces			
Free time in classroom			
Games _____ _____			
Extra recess time			
Food _____ _____			
Pencils			
Erasers			
Special toys			
Small badges			
Special project			
No homework			

Art project			
Game with friend			
Going to Library			
Free reading time			
Trampoline			
Lunch with friend			
Note to parents			
Call to parents			
Popcorn party			
Balloons			
Movie or film time			
Change desk arrangement			
Walk with teacher			
Music/tape player			
Drawing			
Money			
Teacher time			
Special duty			
_____			

ROCKET SHIP #1

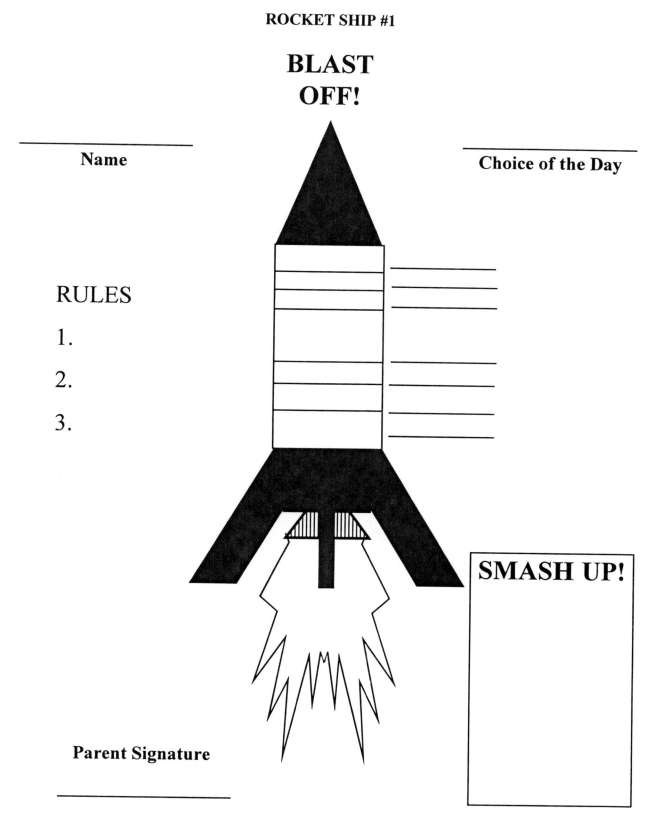

BLAST OFF!

Name

Choice of the Day

RULES

1.

2.

3.

SMASH UP!

Parent Signature

ROCKET SHIP #2

BLAST OFF!

Name _____

Choice of the Day _____

Number of Boxes
for Blast Off:_____

Number of Boxes
Earned:_____

Activity	Rule #1	Rule #2	Rule #3

SMASH UP!

Parent Signature

_____

ROCKET SHIP #3

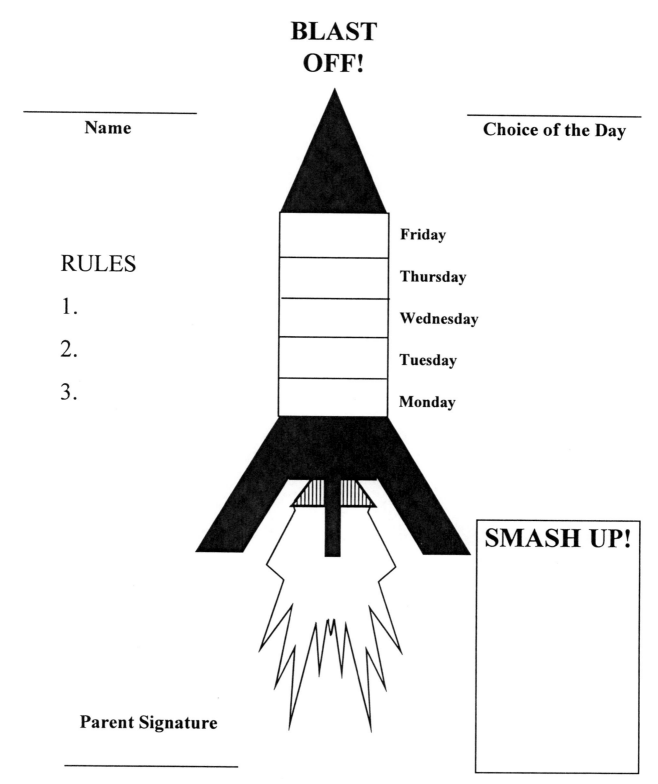

BLAST OFF!

Name

Choice of the Day

RULES

1.

2.

3.

Friday

Thursday

Wednesday

Tuesday

Monday

SMASH UP!

Parent Signature

FLOWER CHART #1

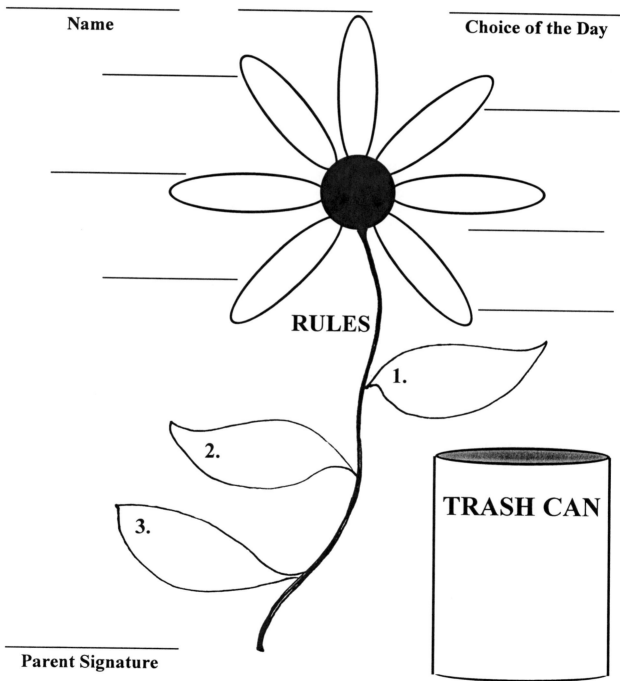

Name

Choice of the Day

RULES

1.

2.

3.

TRASH CAN

Parent Signature

FLOWER CHART #2

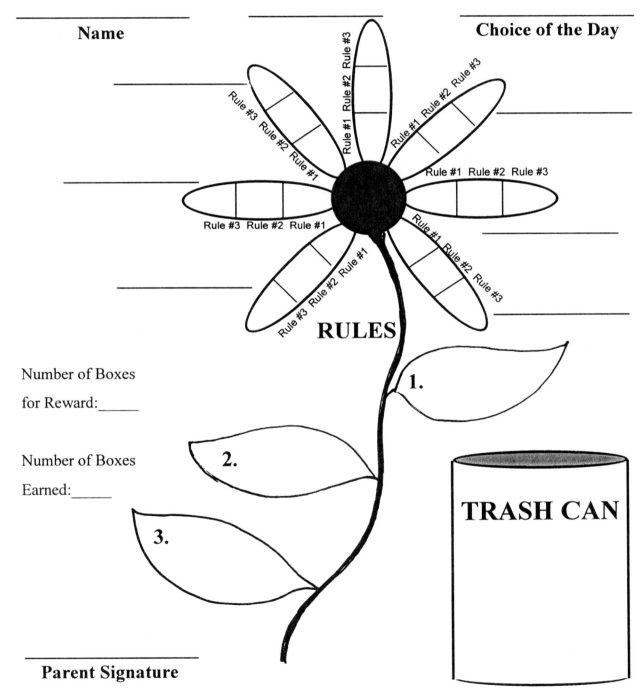

Name

Choice of the Day

Rule #3 Rule #2 Rule #1

Rule #1 Rule #2 Rule #3

Rule #1 Rule #2 Rule #3

Rule #1 Rule #2 Rule #3

Rule #1 Rule #2 Rule #3

Rule #3 Rule #2 Rule #1

Rule #3 Rule #2 Rule #1

RULES

1.

2.

3.

Number of Boxes
for Reward:_____

Number of Boxes
Earned:_____

TRASH CAN

Parent Signature

FLOWER CHART #3

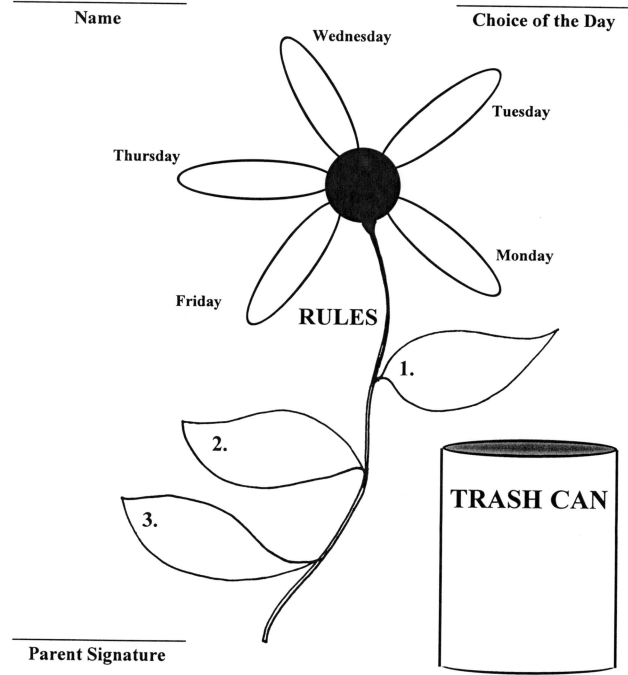

Name

Choice of the Day

Wednesday

Tuesday

Thursday

Monday

Friday

RULES

1.

2.

3.

TRASH CAN

Parent Signature

SNAKE RACE

Name: _____   _____

                                            Choice

Date: _____

RULES:

1.

2.

3.

_____
Parent Signature

PUZZLE PIECE

Name: _____

Date: _____   _____
                                              Reward

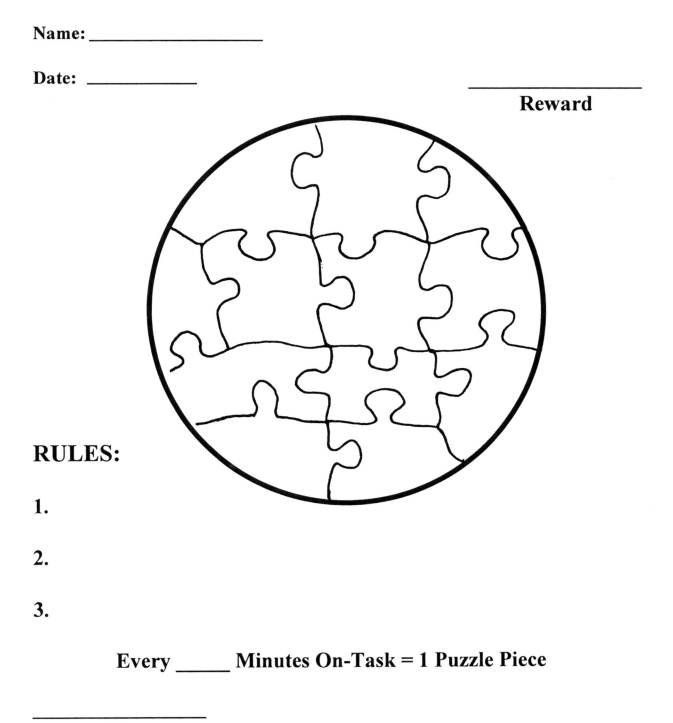

RULES:

1.

2.

3.

Every _____ Minutes On-Task = 1 Puzzle Piece

_____
Parent Signature

Notes

Notes

Notes

Printed in the United States
108536LV00004B/159-250/A